Primary Sources

Other books in the Immigrants in America series:

IMMIGRANTS IN AMERICA

Primary Sources

James D. Torr, *Editor*

Lucent Books, Inc., 10911 Technology Place, San Diego, CA 92127

On Cover:
Immigrants take the oath of citizenship.

Picture Credits
Cover Photo: © Morton Beebe, S. F./CORBIS
© Bettmann/CORBIS, 9, 28, 32, 36, 48, 57, 79
© CORBIS, 13, 21, 23, 38, 41, 51, 72
© Bill Gentile/CORBIS, 85
© Hulton-Deutsch/CORBIS, 43
© Seattle Post-Intelligence Collection; Museum of History &
    Industry/CORBIS, 59
© Dean Wong/CORBIS, 69

Library of Congress Cataloging-in-Publication Data

Torr, James D.
   Primary Sources / ed. James D. Torr
      p. cm. — (Immigrants in America)
Includes bibliographical references (p.) and index.
   Summary: A compilation of articles recalling immigration to
America, discussing reasons for immigration, the process of
starting a new life, hardships of assimilation and discrimination,
and the more recent changes in immigration policy.
ISBN: 1-59018-009-7

Printed in the U.S.A.

CONTENTS

TIMELINE

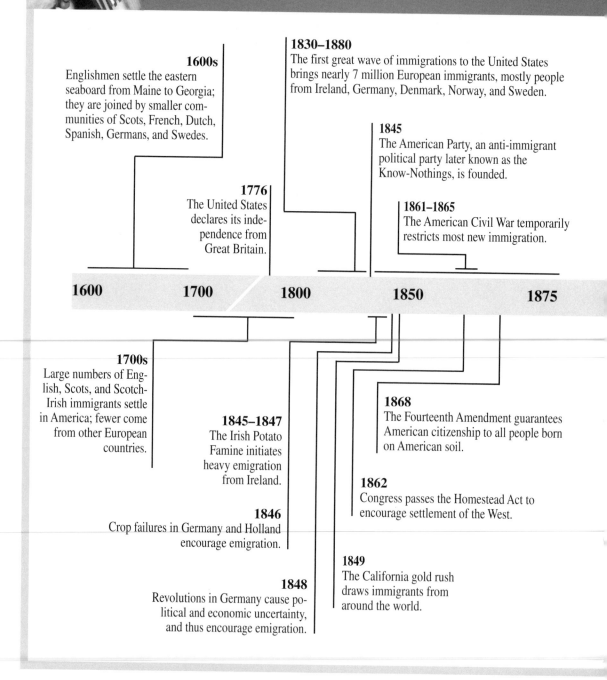

1600s
Englishmen settle the eastern seaboard from Maine to Georgia; they are joined by smaller communities of Scots, French, Dutch, Spanish, Germans, and Swedes.

1830–1880
The first great wave of immigrations to the United States brings nearly 7 million European immigrants, mostly people from Ireland, Germany, Denmark, Norway, and Sweden.

1845
The American Party, an anti-immigrant political party later known as the Know-Nothings, is founded.

1776
The United States declares its independence from Great Britain.

1861–1865
The American Civil War temporarily restricts most new immigration.

| 1600 | 1700 | 1800 | 1850 | 1875 |

1700s
Large numbers of English, Scots, and Scotch-Irish immigrants settle in America; fewer come from other European countries.

1845–1847
The Irish Potato Famine initiates heavy emigration from Ireland.

1868
The Fourteenth Amendment guarantees American citizenship to all people born on American soil.

1846
Crop failures in Germany and Holland encourage emigration.

1862
Congress passes the Homestead Act to encourage settlement of the West.

1848
Revolutions in Germany cause political and economic uncertainty, and thus encourage emigration.

1849
The California gold rush draws immigrants from around the world.

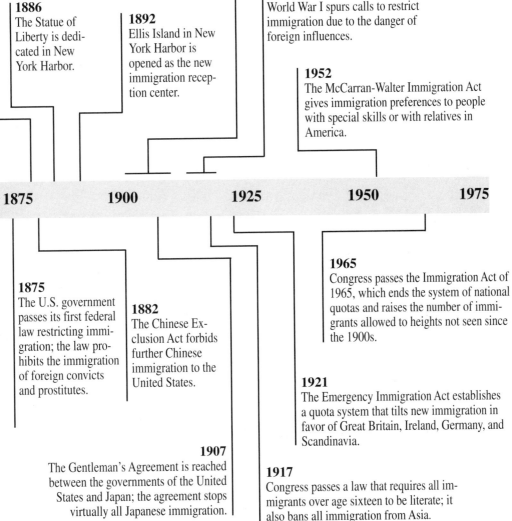

1880
The second great wave of immigrations begins, this time mostly from southern and eastern Europe, Japan, the Philippines, and Mexico.

1901–1910
This is the decade of the heaviest immigration to the United States until the 1980s; it is also the peak decade for Italian immigration.

1886
The Statue of Liberty is dedicated in New York Harbor.

1892
Ellis Island in New York Harbor is opened as the new immigration reception center.

1914–1918
World War I spurs calls to restrict immigration due to the danger of foreign influences.

1952
The McCarran-Walter Immigration Act gives immigration preferences to people with special skills or with relatives in America.

| 1875 | 1900 | 1925 | 1950 | 1975 |

1875
The U.S. government passes its first federal law restricting immigration; the law prohibits the immigration of foreign convicts and prostitutes.

1882
The Chinese Exclusion Act forbids further Chinese immigration to the United States.

1965
Congress passes the Immigration Act of 1965, which ends the system of national quotas and raises the number of immigrants allowed to heights not seen since the 1900s.

1921
The Emergency Immigration Act establishes a quota system that tilts new immigration in favor of Great Britain, Ireland, Germany, and Scandinavia.

1907
The Gentleman's Agreement is reached between the governments of the United States and Japan; the agreement stops virtually all Japanese immigration.

1917
Congress passes a law that requires all immigrants over age sixteen to be literate; it also bans all immigration from Asia.

CHAPTER ONE

Coming to America

Immigrants who come to America do so for a variety of reasons. One of the first groups—the Pilgrims—traveled from England in 1620 seeking religious freedom. Throughout the seventeenth and eighteenth centuries, British immigrants and people of British descent dominated the settlements along the eastern seaboard. Then, from 1775 to 1783, they fought to win their independence from Great Britain and establish the United States of America.

During this time Europe began to experience a population explosion; improvements in agriculture and sanitation allowed more people to live longer. The subsequent increased competition for land and re-sources led many Europeans to America in search of opportunities to work and support themselves. The country, with its vast open spaces, held great appeal for many landless Europeans. In 1818, regular sailing services began between European and American ports, and by 1830, many Europeans were setting out for America.

Between 1830 and 1880 more than 10 million immigrants came to the United States, mostly from Great Britain, Ireland, and Germany. Many of them came to build farms on cheap or free land. As the U.S. economy developed, skilled artisans and businessmen followed, settling in the growing towns and cities of the East Coast.

In 1849 tens of thousands of immigrants, including many Chinese, flocked to California to seek their fortune in the gold rush. Other immigrants came to America to escape problems plaguing their native countries, such as famine, poverty, or political turmoil.

A second great wave of immigration followed from 1880 to 1920, with more than 10 million new immigrants arriving between 1900 and 1910 alone. Since the frontier had largely been settled by 1900, the second wave of immigrants did not have the same access to cheap land. However, because of the Industrial Revolution of the late 1800s, the U.S. economy was booming. In fact, at the turn of the twentieth century, the United States had one of the fastest growing economies in the world.

The second wave was composed mostly of Italians, Greeks, Poles, Czechs, and Russians. Within these groups were hundreds of thousands of European Jews, many of whom were escaping persecution

Second-wave immigrants wait on Ellis Island for a ferry to transport them to New York City.

in Poland and Russia. Japanese immigrants also began to arrive in considerable numbers after their government lifted restriction on emigration, and political problems in Mexico inspired many Mexicans to cross the border during these years.

Although each individual immigrant had his or her own reasons for coming to America, one generalization can be made: They were all seeking a better life for themselves and their children. The documents in this chapter provide further insight into immigrants' motivations.

"Where I Find Bread, There Is My Country"

French writer Michel St. Jean de Crevecoeur lived in the British colonies in North America for several years. Writing during the late eighteenth century, he argued that it was only natural for Europeans to leave the impoverished areas in their home countries for the New World, which de Crevecoeur hailed as a land of plenty. Immigrants, he wrote, should embrace the motto of "Where I find bread, there is my country." De Crevecoeur also proclaimed that the mixing of peoples from all over the world would create in America "a new race of men" that would embrace economic and individual freedom.

What attachment can a poor European emigrant have for a country where he had nothing? The knowledge of the language, the love of a few kindred as poor as himself, were the only cords that tied him: his country is now that which gives him land, bread, protection, and consequence: *Ubi panis ibi patria* ["Where I find bread, there is my country"], is the motto of all emigrants.

What then is the American, this new man? He is either an European, or the descendant of an European, hence that strange mixture of blood, which you will find in no other country. I could point out to you a family whose grandfather was an Englishman, whose wife was Dutch, whose son married a French woman, and whose present four sons have now four wives of different nations. *He* is an American, who leaving behind him all his ancient prejudices and manners, receives new ones from the new mode of life he has embraced, the new government he obeys, and the new rank he holds. He becomes an American by being received in the broad lap of our great *Alma Mater* ["Fostering Mother"]. Here individuals of all nations are melted into a new race of men, whose labours and posterity will one day cause great changes in the world. Americans are the western pilgrims, who are carrying along with them that great mass of arts, sciences, vigour, and industry which began long since in the east; they will finish the great circle. The Americans were once scattered all over Europe; here they are incorporated into one of the finest systems of population which has ever appeared, and which will hereafter become distinct by the power of the different climates they inhabit. The American ought therefore to love this country much better than that wherein either he or his forefathers were born. Here the rewards of his industry follow with equal steps the progress of his labour; his labour is founded on the basis of nature, *self-interest;* can it want a stronger allurement? Wives and children, who before in vain demanded of him a morsel of bread, now, fat and frolicsome, gladly help their father to clear those fields whence exuberant crops are to arise to feed and to clothe them all; without any part being claimed, either by a despotic prince, a rich abbot, or a mighty lord.

Michel St. Jean de Crevecoeur, *Letters from an American Farmer*. New York: Foxx, Duffield, 1904.

 ### Luring People into Indentured Servitude

During the seventeenth and eighteenth centuries, a significant portion of English immigrants to America were indentured servants. These workers signed contracts to work for a number of years (usually five), and in exchange they received free passage to the British colonies in America. Advertisements in London tried to attract new indentured servants by describing life in the British colonies as an adventure. In his 1770 letter home to England, excerpted below, immigrant William Eddis seeks to expose this lie. He writes that the lot of indentured servants was little better than that of slaves.

In your frequent excursions about the great metropolis [London], you cannot but observe numerous advertisements, offering the most seducing encouragement to adventurers under every possible description; to those who are disgusted with the frowns of fortune in their native land; and to those of an enterprising disposition, who are tempted to court her smiles in a distant region [the British colonies in America]. These persons are referred to agents, or crimps, who represent the advantages to be obtained in America, in colours so alluring, that it is almost impossible to resist their artifices [lies]. Unwary persons are accordingly induced to enter into articles [contracts], by which they engage to become servants, agreeable to their respective qualifications, for the term of five years; every necessary accommodation being found [provided to] them during the voyage; and every method taken that they may be treated with tenderness and humanity during the period of servitude; at the expiration of which they are taught to expect, that opportunities will assuredly offer to secure to the honest and industrious, a competent provision for the remainder of their days.

[People here in the colonies] are very little acquainted with those fallacious [false] pretences, by which numbers are continually induced to embark for this continent. . . . Nor will they readily believe that people, who had the least experience in life, and whose characters were unexceptionable, would abandon their friends and families, and their ancient connexions [connections], for a servile situation, in a remote appendage to the British Empire. . . . Negroes being a property for life, the death of slaves, in the prime of youth or strength, is a material loss to the proprietor; they are, therefore, almost in every instance, under more comfortable circumstances than the miserable European, over whom the rigid planter exercises an inflexible severity. They [European servants] are strained to the utmost to perform their allotted labour. . . . For real, or imaginary causes, these frequently attempt to escape, but very few are successful; the country being intersected with rivers, and the utmost vigilance observed in detecting persons under suspicious circumstances, who, when apprehended, are committed to close confinement, advertised, and delivered to their respective masters; the party who detects the vagrant being entitled to a reward. Other incidental charges arise. The unhappy culprit is doomed to a severe chastisement [punishment].

William Eddis, *Letters from America*. Ed. by Aubrey C. Land. Cambridge, MA: Belknap Press of Harvard University Press, 1969.

"No Poor" and "Very Few Crimes"

In this 1796 letter to an English newspaper, Joseph Priestley, a renowned scientist and Unitarian minister, describes what he considers to be the benefits of immigrating to America. Priestley's claim that there are "no poor" in America is certainly false, but his letter does provide insight into the political and economic motivations of many middle-class, late-eighteenth-century European immigrants. Priestley emphasizes America's low taxes and its lack of an established church—a contrast to conditions in his native England, where citizens paid high taxes to the monarchy and to the established Church of England.

My dear sir,
Every account I have from England makes me think myself happy in this peaceful retirement, where I enjoy almost every thing I can wish in this life. . . .

The advantages we enjoy in this country [America] are indeed very great. Here we have no poor; we never see a beggar, nor is there a family in want. We have no church establishment, and hardly any taxes. [The country] pays all its officers from a treasure in the public funds. There are very few crimes committed, and we travel without the least apprehension of danger. The press is perfectly free, and I hope we shall always keep out of war.

I do not think there ever was any country in a state of such rapid improvement as this present; but we have not the same advantages for literary and philosophical pursuits that you have in Europe, though even in this respect we are every day getting better. Many books are now printing here, but what scholars chiefly want are old books, and these are not to be had. . . .

With every good wish to my country and to yourself, I am, dear sir,
Your's sincerely,
J. PRIESTLEY.

Joseph Priestley, Letter to a Leeds Newspaper, October 4, 1796.

An Irish Immigrant Praises American Liberty

Although the greatest wave of Irish immigration to the United States occurred in the wake of the 1840s potato famine, many Irishmen did leave their homeland before the 1840s. One reason they did so was the harshness and cruelty with which Great Britain ruled Ireland during the nineteenth century. In an 1818 letter home to his wife, excerpted below, Irish immigrant John Doyle emphasizes the political freedom enjoyed by immigrants to the United States.

As yet it's only natural I should feel lonesome in this country, ninety-nine out of every hundred who come to it are at first disappointed. . . . Still, it's a fine country and a much better place for a poor man than Ireland . . . and much as they grumble at first, after a while they never think of leaving it. . . . One thing I think is certain, that if emigrants knew beforehand what they have to suffer for about the first six months after leaving home in every respect, they would never come here. However, an enterprising man, desirous of advancing himself in the world, will despise everything for coming to this free country, where a man is allowed to thrive and flourish without having a penny taken out of his pocket by government; no visits from tax gatherers, constables or soldiers, every one

During the nineteenth century, many Irish families, fleeing severe poverty and oppressive English rule, immigrated to America.

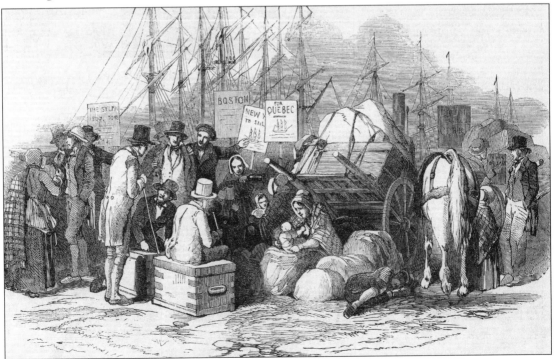

at liberty to act and speak as he likes, provided he does not hurt another, to slander and damn government, abuse public men in their office to their faces, wear your hat in court and smoke a cigar while speaking to the judge as familiarly as if he was a common mechanic, hundreds go unpunished for crimes for which they would be surely hung in Ireland; in fact they are so tender of life in this country that a person should have a very great interest to get himself hanged for anything.

William D. Griffin, comp. and ed., *The Irish in America, 1550–1972: A Chronology & Fact Book*. Dobbs Ferry, NY: Oceana Publications, 1973.

Economic Opportunities Draw Skilled Craftsmen

The economic opportunities America has to offer have always been one of the most important factors in attracting immigrants to the United States. The experience of Edward Phillips reflects this. Phillips, a cotton handloom weaver, came to the United States alone in 1817 at the age of forty-five, because there was much greater demand for his skills in America. His family followed him only after he had established himself in his trade. In these two letters home to his brother, excerpted below, Phillips emphasizes not only the economic success he achieved in America, but also the religious freedom and the democratic government that Americans enjoy.

Dear Brother,

I embrace this opportunity of writing to you hoping this will find you, my brother Thomas, and John in good health, and their families. I got to Liverpool [England] on the 23rd of August after parting with you. I sailed from there on the 7th of September. . . . We landed in New York on the 17th of October, left there for Philadelphia, got there on the 20th, went to work the day after with a farmer, where I remained six weeks. Then I got employment in my own business in Philadelphia. I came to this place on the 12th day of last August; this is a small village in the State of Delaware, six miles from Wilmington, and 34 from Philadelphia. Trade here is rather dull, yet my employer has kindly agreed to send for my family, by giving a note for 31 pounds 10 shillings British, which is the cheapest passage I could get. . . . The merchant tells me that he expects they will be here in four months from this time. My wife sent me word that they would be assisted . . . to pay their expenses to Liverpool, yet . . . I am afraid they will be ill provided to prepare for themselves, as they must be badly off for clothing. Dear brother, if you would send them a trifle [a little money] you would ever oblige me and them; and it should be gratefully acknowledged, and returned as soon as possible after. . . . My two sons that are married are likely to be left behind at present; but with the help of God I hope it will be in my power to send for them soon. . . .

I like this country [America] very well for many reasons, particularly the attention paid to Religion, and the freedom a man may use in adoring his Maker in his own way. I have known them in the city of

Philadelphia to put chains across the street at time of service to prevent coaches or carts from disturbing the congregation. I conclude by giving my best love to you my brother and all friends, wishing you all every happiness, both spiritual and temporal. Such is the ardent wish of your ever affectionate Brother,
EDWARD PHILLIPS

Dear Brother,

I take this opportunity of writing to you, and I hope these few lines will find you in good health, as it leaves me and mine. They [my family] landed at Philadelphia the 15th of June, all in good health, after a passage of 49 days. I got to hear of the vessel going up the river, and was in Philadelphia the day after they landed, which is a distance of forty miles, and was happy to see them all in good health—happier than I can express in words to see them all well after an absence of nearly three years. . . . I am much indebted to you for your kindness in assisting my family to come to me. . . . As for your son, if you should send him I will use him as one of my own. As I intend sending for my two sons next spring you can have an opportunity of sending him along with them. And if my brother John thinks of coming, let them all come together.

The Government in this country I think is excellent. In the first place the people have the chusing [choice] of all the Governors from the constable to the President. The Magistrates are chiefly the working class of people, and are chosen annually. As there is no established religion there are no tithes [taxes], and every profession pay their own clergy. We are comfortably situated here, markets [prices] are low. . . .

No more at present, from your affectionate brother and sister,
EDWARD AND M. PHILLIPS

Letters from Edward Phillips to England, 1820–1845.

 Reports of the Irish Potato Famine

The Irish Potato Famine of 1845–1849 was the most severe famine to occur in nineteenth-century Europe. It was also the principal reason approximately 1.4 million Irish immigrated to the United States between 1846 and 1854. The famine was caused by a plant disease called blight that destroyed the potato crop over the course of several years. In a country where half the population depended on potatoes for sustenance, the blight resulted in more than 1 million deaths from starvation and from the spread of typhus and other diseases brought on by malnutrition and weakness. The following description of the devastation the famine caused in Ireland is by James Mahoney, a writer who reported on the famine for Irish and British newspapers in 1847.

I started from Cork . . . for Skibbereen and saw little until we came to Clonakilty, where the coach stopped for breakfast; and here, for the first time, the horrors of the poverty became visible, in the vast number of famished poor, who flocked around the coach to beg alms [charity]: amongst them was a woman carrying in her arms the corpse of a fine child, and making the most distressing appeal to the passengers for aid to enable her to purchase a coffin and bury her dear little baby. This horrible spectacle induced me to make some inquiry about her, when I learned from the people of the hotel that each day brings dozens of such applicants into the town.

After leaving Clonakilty, each step that we took westward brought fresh evidence of the truth of the reports of the misery, as we either met a funeral or a coffin at every hundred yards, until we approached the country of the Shepperton Lakes. Here, the distress became more striking, from the decrease of numbers at the funerals, none having more than eight or ten attendants, and many only two or three.

We next reached Skibbereen. . . . I can now, with perfect confidence, say that neither pen nor pencil ever could portray the misery and horror, at this moment, to be witnessed in Skibbereen. We first proceeded to Bridgetown . . . and there I saw the dying, the living, and the dead, lying indiscriminately upon the same floor, without anything between them and the cold earth, save a few miserable rags upon them. To point to any particular house as a proof of this would be a waste of time, as all were in the same state; and, not a single house out of 500 could boast of being free from death and fever, though several could be pointed out with the dead lying close to the living for the space of three or four, even six days, without any effort being made to remove the bodies to a last resting place.

We next got to Skull, where, by the attention of Dr. Traill, vicar of the parish (and whose humanity at the present moment is beyond all praise), we witnessed almost indescribable in-door horrors. In the street, however, we had the best opportunity of judging of the condition of the people; for here, from three to five hundred women, with money in their hands, were seeking to buy food; whilst a few of the Government officers doled out Indian meal to them in their turn. . . . One of the women told me she had been standing there since daybreak, seeking to get food for her family at home.

This food, it appeared, was being doled out in miserable quantities, at 'famine prices,' to the neighbouring poor, from a stock lately arrived in a sloop [boat], with a Government steamship to protect its cargo of 50 tons; whilst the population amounts to 27,000; so that you may calculate what were the feelings of the disappointed mass.

James Mahoney, Sketches in the West of Ireland, February 13, 1847.

Stories of Success Encourage Others to Immigrate

Many Scandinavian emigrants left for America between 1840 and 1880 to escape the poverty of their native countries. Like other immigrant groups, they wrote home, telling friends, family, and neighbors of their successes and failures. Success stories of early immigrants, such as the two excerpted below, were a major factor in in-

fluencing friends and family at home to come to America.

Part I

The soil here is as fertile as any you can find in America, and our daily food consists of rye and wheat bread, bacon, butter, eggs, molasses, sugar, coffee, and beer. The corn that grows on large cobs is rarely eaten by people; it is not tender enough for that, but is used as fodder for the animals. Thus you can understand that we have had no trouble making a living and have not had to ask others for help. My brothers and sisters and I have all acquired land, and we are happy and content. This year we have produced so much foodstuff that we have been able to sell instead of having to buy, and we all have cattle, driving oxen, and wagons. We also have children in abundance. Gunild has given birth to two girls, Sigri and Anne, and I have also had two here, a boy called Terje and a girl called Sigri. But Ole and Joraand have no children.

Our old father, who is in good health, received the $200 in June. My sister Sigri worked for twenty-five weeks in a town forty miles from here and got $25 for that. Guro has traveled thirty-five miles from here down to Koshkonong Prairie to be confirmed; she will not return till next spring.

Since I love you, Tellef, more than all my other brothers and sisters, I feel very sorry that you have to work your youth away in Norway, where it is so difficult to get ahead. There you can't see any results

of your labor, while here you can work ahead to success and get to own a good deal of property, even though you did not have a penny to begin with. I wish that you would sell the farm now for what you can get for it and come here as fast as possible. I and all the others with me believe that you would not regret it. Our old father would tell you the same thing. He has heard that you do not feel like leaving, and he says that you are so young and inexperienced that it may be best for you to try your luck in Norway first. Then later you will be very glad to come here. If you do come, we hope that you will not be so foolish as to go to the warm Texas. It is true that Reiersen praises it highly, but when my mother asked him how conditions were in Texas, he himself told her that it was so hot there that if you put a pan with bacon out on the street, it fries by itself. Then, of course, we were frightened at the thought of such a hot climate and were afraid to go there. And when they say in Texas that a man can get a completely satisfying meal out of a cob of corn, we conclude that this must be because the people there are so sickly and unhealthy that they cannot eat very much. We are to blame for not having written about this before, but the reason was that we had not expected that our brothers and sisters would want to go to Texas. We are a little surprised to see that our relatives do not seem to love us so very much, since they want to travel to such a remote place, as if they were afraid of meeting us again. But it is just the same to us; if they can get along without us, we can get along without them, but I do know that none of us would have acted in this way. We have talked to a man by the name of Kjøstel, from Holt, who had traveled far into Texas with Jørgen Hasle, but when he saw the way people lived there he returned. They have neither wheat bread nor butter there, only the coarse corn foodstuff, but we here in Wisconsin would not be satisfied with such hog's feed.

Part II

I must take this opportunity to let you know that we are in the best of health, and that we—both my wife and I—find ourselves exceedingly satisfied. Our son attends the English school, and talks English as well as the native born. Nothing has made me more happy and contented than the fact that we left Norway and journeyed to this country. We have gained more since our arrival here than I did during all the time that I lived in Norway, and I have every prospect of earning a livelihood here for myself and my family—even if my family were larger—so long as God gives me good health.

Such excellent plans have been developed here that, even though one be infirm, no one need suffer want. Competent men are elected whose duty it is to see that no needy persons, either in the cities or in the country, shall have to beg for their living. If a man dies and is survived by a widow and children who are unable to support themselves—as is so often the case—they have the privilege of petitioning these officials. To each one will then be given every year as much as is needed of clothes and food, and no discrimination will be shown between the native-born and those from foreign countries. These things I have learned through daily observation, and I do not believe there can be better laws and arrangements . . . in the whole world. I have talked with a sensible person who has traveled in many countries, who has lived here twenty-six years, and has a full knowledge of the matter; both of him and of other reliable persons I have made inquiries, for I wish to let everyone know the truth.

When assemblies are held to elect officials who are to serve the country, the vote of the common man carries just as much authority and influence as does that of the rich and powerful man. Neither in the matter of clothes nor in seats are distinctions to be observed, whether one be a farmer or a clerk. The freedom which one enjoys is just as good as that of the other. So long as he comports himself honestly [behaves properly] he will be subjected to no interference. Everybody has the liberty to travel about in the country, wherever he wishes, without any passports or papers. Everyone is permitted to engage in whatever business he finds most desirable, in trade or commerce, by land or by water. But if anyone is found guilty of crime, he will be prosecuted and severely punished for it.

No duties are levied upon goods which are produced in the country and brought to the city by water or by land. In case of death, no registration is required; the survivor, after paying the debts, is free to dispose of the property for himself and his family just as he desires. . . . It would heartily please me if I could learn that every one of you who are in need and have little chance of gaining support for yourselves and your families would make up your mind to leave Norway and come to America, for, even if many more were to come, there would still be room here for all. For all those who are willing to work there is no lack of employment and business here. It is possible for all to live in comfort and without suffering want. I do not believe that any of those who suffer under the oppression of others and who must rear their children under straitened [difficult, strained] circumstances could do better than to help the latter to come to America. But alas, many persons, even though they want to come, lack the necessary means and many others are so stupid as to believe that it is best to live in the country where they have been brought up even if they have nothing but hard bread to satisfy their hunger. It is as if they should say that those who move to a better land, where there is plenty, commit a wrong. But I can find no place where our Creator has forbidden one to seek one's food in an honorable manner. I should like to talk to many persons in Norway for a little while, but we do not wish to live in Norway. We lived there altogether too long. Nor have I talked with any immigrant in this country who wished to return.

Part I: Theodore C. Blegen, ed., *The Land of Their Choice: The Immigrants Write Home*. Minneapolis: University of Minnesota Press, 1955. Part II: Martin Ridge and Ray Allen Billington, eds., *America's Frontier Story: A Documentary History of Westward Expansion*. New York: Holt, Rinehart, and Winston, 1969.

Crossing the Atlantic

In the following passage from a letter home, German immigrant Gerhard Kremers describes in great detail his family's journey across the Atlantic Ocean to New York. Kremers writes that during the voyage the food was awful and seasickness was rampant, but that on the whole the experience was not as perilous as he had imagined.

Following the painful day of separations, we took the train the next morning at Duisburg which brought us to Bremen the same evening. After a lapse of three days we went to Bremerhaven, where the anchors were weighed on the 19th of April. With good cheer and favorable wind we sailed down the ever widening Weser [river] into the North sea. A truly great spectacle: the unbounded expanse of the sea makes an unforgettable impression on the admirer. However, the very next morning the sight had lost its sublimity [splendor] for many. With a strong wind, which enabled us to make four [knots] per hour, the disagreeable seasickness made its appearance. Though by no means dangerous, it is accompanied by a sense of annoyance. Since this sickness has been described so often, it would be superfluous to describe it in detail though I could write from experience. Children are not affected, also some grown ups, among them my father. . . .

A few days later we had to entrust ourselves to the waves of the Atlantic ocean, which were readily recognized by their size. The wind became less strong and for 8–10 days we made little progress. But now there came a change. Suddenly toward evening a wind arose. It became stronger and stronger and bulged the sails. Waves 25 feet high crowded each other while their spray was carried away by the wind and struck with hissing sounds. Our small ship, which had only 130 passengers on board, tilted to the side so that occasionally the railing was on a level with the surface of the water. However, it made great progress. . . . Trunks, tin containers, and other objects fell over. The dreadfulness was increased by the darkness of the night and the phosphorescence [glow] of the sea. The whole was of such a nature, that, as the sailors told us, we might get a fair idea of a storm, but that it could not be called such. Toward morning it became more quiet. Even in worse storms the voyage on the open sea is not dangerous though it is so near the coast. Anyone who desires to emigrate will not be induced to give up his plans because of such contingencies. Moreover, accidents are very rare. Should there be sufficient cause, we should not hesitate to entrust ourselves to the waves again. . . .

Before proceeding, I shall say something about our provisions on board ship. Our food was very poor: poor coffee, poor pork, and malodorous [smelly] beef; in addition we received bread, butter, peas, beans, barley, and rice. Even these would not have been edible because of poor preparation had not hunger spiced the meals. Several modest requests for a better preparation of the food were rejected in a harsh voice. This incivility we could bear so long as our own provisions lasted. These exhausted, our patience had an end. Several of our traveling companions informed the captain in all seriousness that he had to provide better food. This decisive demand produced results. Whether angry or frightened, I know not, but the captain changed color several times. From now on we, the passengers, prepared our own food. So far as the material, delivered in sufficient quantity, was concerned it was good, the dishes prepared there were palatable. However, such supplies as were poor to begin with could not be improved. Owner, captain, and cook all three were to blame. . . .

But now let us return to the American coast which we approached very closely. . . . Every one was jubilant over our early arrival in the country which our eyes had sought so eagerly and so often. While Long Island [New York] spread out to our right, we could see the endless main land to our south. However, as we came closer, all was hidden by a dense fog. Night overtook us and the ship dropped its anchor. As the fog disappeared the next morning, we saw land close by. Words fail to describe how happy we were. It was as though winter had suddenly been replaced by spring. On both sides beautiful panorama delighted the eye. On both sides beautiful knolls covered with a variety of trees and studded with country homes. At the foot of the hills white houses, one more beautiful than the other. Of interest also are the fortresses with their cannons. Before us and to our rear hundreds of masts of ships from all parts of the world. In addition, steamships, very different from the German ones, cross the bay. . . . [Every one] was happy over the fortunate termination of our trip. . . . After a rapid and none too strict inspection of our baggage, and after the physician had done his duty, toward noon of the 37th day we were conveyed by a steamer to New York. An endless forest of masts of sailing vessels and of smoke stacks of the largest steamers stretches along the shore line of the city. Presumably but few cities afford a like sight. The impression made upon us was great.

Gerhard Kremers, *An Immigrant Letter,* Manitowoc Rapids, in the State of Wisconsin, July 26, 1848.

German "Forty-Eighter" Finds Freedom in America

While many immigrants came to America seeking economic opportunity, others were motivated by the political freedom the United States offered. Many German immigrants came to America after a series of revolutions in 1848 failed to bring democracy to Germany. One such immigrant, Carl Schurz, wrote a friend at home in 1855 that he believed the prospects for freedom were better in the United States than Germany.

As long as there is no upheaval of affairs in Europe it is my firm resolve to regard this

In this political cartoon, Uncle Sam, who represents America, welcomes immigrants seeking political freedom.

country not as a transient or accidental abode, but as the field for my usefulness. I love America and I am vitally interested in the things about me—they no longer seem strange. I find that the question of liberty is in its essence the same everywhere, however different its form. Although I do not regard the public affairs of this country with the same devotion as those of our old home, it is not mere ambition nor eagerness for distinction that impels me to activity. My interest in the political contests of this country is so strong, so spontaneous, that I am profoundly stirred. More self-control is required for me to keep aloof than to participate in them. These are the years of my best strength. . . .

I feel that here I can accomplish something. I am convinced of it when I consider the qualities of the men who are now conspicuous. This inspires me, and even if the prospects of success did not correspond with my natural impulses, I should suddenly find that I had involuntarily entered into the thick of the fight. In these circumstances, why should I wish to return to Europe? I am happy that I have a firm foothold and good opportunities. . . .

I expect to go to Wisconsin. I transferred some of my business interests there when on my last trip to the West. The German element is powerful in that State, the immigrants being so numerous, and they are striving for political recognition. They only lack leaders that are not bound by the restraints of money-getting. There is the place where I can find a sure, gradually expanding field for my work without truckling [submitting] to the nativistic elements, and there, I hope, in time, to gain influence that may also become useful to our cause. It is my belief that the future interests of America and Germany are closely interwoven. The two countries will be natural allies as soon as a European upheaval takes place. However different the two nations may be in character, they will have the same opponents, and that will compel them to have a corresponding foreign policy. American influence in Europe will be based on Germany, and Germany's world-position will depend essentially on the success of America. Germany is the only power in Europe whose interests will not conflict with those of America, and America is the only power in the civilized world that would not be jealous of a strong, united Germany. They can both grow without being rivals, and it will be to the interest of each to keep the adversaries of the other in check. Americans will realize this as soon as the Emperor of Austria and the King of Prussia need no longer be considered, and the Germans will become convinced of it as soon as they consider a national foreign policy.

Moses Rischin, ed., *Immigration and the American Tradition*. Indianapolis: Bobbs-Merrill. 1976.

Deceived into Coming to America

Toward the end of the nineteenth century, skilled workers in the United States began organizing into unions to bargain for higher wages. In response, employers tried to persuade skilled artisans in Europe, whom they hoped they could pay lower wages, to come to America. One such immigrant was Johann Rosinger, an Austrian artisan who was treated poorly by employers after coming to America in 1881. This selection is excerpted from a letter Rosinger wrote to a German-language newspaper, warning his countrymen not to be deceived as he was.

In November of the year 1881, I was urged to travel to America by the slave trader, Jaburek. He made me the most glittering promises. I am a meerschaum [a white clayey mineral] and amber worker by trade, and during my stay in Vienna [Austria] I worked for four years in one of the largest Viennese factories, where I made a so-called good living.

Nevertheless, I let myself be deceived by the scoundrel and have been paying bitterly for it ever since. I was sent by the agent across the ocean on a steamship, and after a stormy twenty-two day trip, I arrived in New York where my distant fate awaited me. No one fetched me in New York, though Jaburek had promised me that someone would find me a job and a place to live as soon as I got there. But that was all part of the swindle. Jaburek just wanted to stick me with a 120 Mark ticket, and in this he succeeded. Like many of my comrades in suffering, I was lured here to compete with the other workers. After three weeks I finally found work with Karl Weiss in New York, where I was supposed to make $13.00 a week. But my problems

New York City construction workers organize to gain better wages. Many American employers used immigrant labor to replace union workers.

had only begun. Weiss was going to deduct one dollar a week, so that, as he put it, he could give me the money at the end of the year. I wouldn't hear of it and was let go. Here and there I found part-time work with masters in small shops and in this way just managed to eke out a living.

I was informed by Mr. Benzinger in New York that a Mr. Metzler had written him; he and a Mr. Rothschild wanted him to send meerschaum and amber cutters to Chicago. Travel costs were to be reimbursed and the salary was said to be good. At that time I was completely out of work. A few people from Vienna took me into their care and got together the money necessary for me to buy a train ticket to Chicago. I had already been warned about Mssrs Metzler and Rothschild's foreman in New York. I didn't like him from the very start, and he acted hostilely toward me. He made trouble in order to get me to work for less and then offered me $10.00 a week. I demanded $12.00. He said the business turned little profit, which was new to me, since the owners were millionaires and the workers beggars. He finally gave me $12.00, but at the same time he wrote to New York for another worker. Eight days before Christmas I was let go. This clearly illustrates the capitalists' ruthlessness. I was thrown out on the pavement without a penny in my pocket, no friends, no relatives, starving and freezing. For eight full weeks I led a wretched existence. No work and no pay anywhere, and if I hadn't had so much endurance, I would long since have put an end to all my misery and suffering. . . .

Publish these lines . . . , Mr. Editor, so that my countrymen will not be swindled and driven into the arms of poverty as have been I and so many others.

A Letter to the Editor from an Immigrant Meerschaum and Amber Cutter, *Chicagoer Arbeiter-Zeitung*, February 6, 1883.

The Lure of Cheap Land

For many immigrants, one of the main attractions of America was the widespread availability of land. In Europe, land ownership was restricted to the aristocracy, but in nineteenth-century America there were countless acres waiting to be settled. In 1862 the U.S. government passed the Homestead Act, which made much of the land in the Great Plains free to anyone willing to farm it for five years. A flood of immigrants from Scandinavia and eastern and central Europe poured in to help develop America's emerging breadbasket. In this letter to home, a Swedish immigrant described how happy he was in his new home.

Much I have seen, heard, and experienced, but nothing unhappy, no shady sides. To be sure I believed when I departed from home, from the fatherland, from family, friends, and acquaintances, that everything would at first be rather unfamiliar. But no, strangely enough, everything is as I wished it should be. The country is beautiful, if any land on earth deserves to be called so. And if you compare conditions here with Sweden's, there is no similarity at all. The soil consists of a kind of dark loam [clayey dirt] over a layer of marl [loose, sandy dirt] on a clay base; your finest plowlands at home cannot compare with the rich prairies here, where golden harvests grow from year to year without having to be manured or ditched. No stones, no stumps hinder the cultivator's plow. If you add to this that one can almost get such land as a gift or for an insignificant sum compared with its natural value, you soon have an idea why America is truly and undeniably better than old Sweden. But here is another thing, taxes do not consume the American farmer, they are extremely light. America maintains no expensive royal house, no inactive armies, which undermine the people's welfare; such things are considered here as superfluous articles and extremely harmful. Never has a freer people trodden, cultivated, and tended a better land than this. Hundreds of thousands of persons have found here the happiness they vainly sought in Europe's lands.

The greater part have come here without means, many even with debts. But with good will and an unshakable will to work they have within a few years gradually attained sustenance, prosperity, indeed quite often wealth. And still there is land for a hundred million people, as fabulous as this may sound. In twelve years the population of Nebraska has increased from thirty thousand to four hundred thousand; no other place in America can show such rapid growth. Swedes number around fifteen thousand in Nebraska. All are getting along well, and when you are getting along well you are not likely to long for what

was not pleasant; even homesickness is fully cured. And as far as food is concerned, there is such great abundance here that one would be amazed, even if he were the greatest gourmet. To list everything here would surely be too long; let me therefore say that it is unfamiliar to us Swedes. Now someone may perhaps believe that there are bad persons and dangerous beasts here, but there is neither. When we arrived we heard from everyone's lips, welcome, heartily welcome, and they showed by their actions that they meant what they said; they invited us to eat as though we had been their nearest relatives. My traveling companion has bought eighty acres or tunnland of land for around fifty dollars. The climate is remarkably fine; nothing stands in our way except the language. We cannot understand their speech, but it is possible for us to learn as well as others have done. I see after this first short time that it is going well. And therefore you can understand that I do not regret the journey, other than to regret that I had not made it before. But better late than never, as the saying goes, and I agree.

C.F. Carlsson, Letter to Dalarna, early 1880s.

 ### Destitute Hungarians Seek a Better Life

By 1879, as the numbers of immigrants arriving from Europe reached record numbers, the New York Times *began reporting regularly on the new arrivals, the ships that brought them, and their ports of origin. In*

the following selection the Times *highlighted the arrival of a group of Hungarians who left their homeland because of devastating floods. These immigrants arrived at Castle Garden in southern Manhattan, which served as the chief processing center for new immigrants before Ellis Island. The* Times *reported the views of the superintendent of Castle Garden, who expected to see many more Hungarian immigrants as recent arrivals sent home for their families.*

The arrivals of immigrants at Castle Garden since Saturday, are as follows: Per City of Berlin, Liverpool, 354; Elysin, London, 53; Spain, Liverpool, 255; Mass, Rotterdam, 135; Anchoria, Glasgow, 177; total, 974. Among this number of Hungarians, who arrived in a destitute condition. Thirty of these people came last week, and had immediately to be taken charge of, by the Castle Garden officers. Superintendent Jackson finally found employment for them at Lenhardtsville, Bucks County, in the lumber region of Pennsylvania. They were all woodchoppers and hardy forest laborers, hence the reason for sending them there. Yesterday, the *Spain* discharged 90 more of these people, equally destitute, on the Emigration Department. The astonished officers became alarmed, and instituted inquiries. It was not easy to communicate with the men, as they could not speak English, French, or German; but an interpreter was found with some trouble. It was learned that they had come from the flooded districts of Hungary, where the crops have failed and long continued rains have caused the inundation of the country, sweeping away the subsistence of the people. The immigrants sold everything they had to get money enough to pay their passage to this country, which was necessarily expensive as they had to come from the interior of Hungary, through Germany, to Liverpool. The section they come from rejoices in the unpronounceable name of Sarosmegye. They are all lumbermen and farmers. It is exceedingly likely that the steerage fare on the *Spain* was the best feeding they ever had in their lives. They were landed looking strong and hearty, but without so much as a rent among the whole lot, and they had to get their breakfast from the department people in whose charge they for the present will remain. Superintendent Jackson says they are honest, hard-working fellows, and he thinks there will not be much difficulty to find work for them; but he says what he rather dreads is, that when they have got $15 or $20 together, each man will be sending for his family, and a long string of equally destitute Hungarian wives and children will trail through the department for a year or more.

Ethnic Groups in American Life. New York: Arno Press and the *New York Times*, 1978.

Fleeing War and Genocide

Many immigrants made a deliberate choice to come to America and build a new life. Many less fortunate people, however, were forced to emigrate from their home countries in order to survive. This was the case for many Jewish refugees who came to America to escape the Holocaust. Genocide also forced many Armenians to flee their homeland in Turkey between 1894 and 1896, and then again during World War I. In the following passage, Leo Hamalian describes the "survivor guilt" that his father, an Armenian, experienced after leaving Turkey in 1911 to come to America. Hamalian writes that his father never really embraced being an American because he felt guilty over escaping the genocide that killed his family and so many of his countrymen.

My father, like most Armenian survivors of the Turkish genocide, was a man who never wanted to leave home. Until he was forced to flee, he loved the place where he had been born and brought up. It was a milieu [environment] alien to the American mentality, and as a result my father never really adapted to the customs of this country. As I look back upon his memory, more in sadness then in the anger I used to feel flaring so often in his presence, I think that his life was about the damage done to the human spirit by exile.

From the time that he set foot in the New World in 1911, an early victim of the Turkish pogroms [organized massacres] against Christians, to the day of his lonely death in 1939, neither the chimera [fantasy] of the American Dream nor the bounty of material rewards could numb the pain of a refugee who found himself uprooted in a strange land where he was forced to flourish or founder. He [never felt] all those things that transformed other transplanted Armenians into lovers of this land. . . .

He must have left recognizing the grim shadow that the future threw before him. Of a large family of prosperous peasants in the Lake Van area, only he and his sister got out of Turkey before the Turks got them, he to America, she to Egypt, where she lived out her days as a stateless person. . . .

He tried to be a good American as he understood the idea. He became a photo-engraver, took his family to picnics in [New York's] Hudson Park, argued politics while he played backgammon with his cronies, attended church on 34th street, and perhaps hoped that the Big Dream would materialize, as it did for so many other Armenians. Instead, I suspect, it only emphasized his sense of loss. His emotional attachment to the place that had treated him like dirt was so massive, so monumental that he was almost blind to the bounty he had reaped in his new homeland.

Why did he resist resurrection when other Armenians were rising out of the ashes of the Turkish tragedy? I am not sure I know, but I think that the stone of sorrow in his guts may simply have stayed stone. Nothing softened it, and his stonified sorrow showed itself in excessive sternness with his children. The more American we became, the more infuriated he became. We couldn't tell whether his anger was directed against America or against us. We felt that we had somehow misbehaved by becoming what we had to become in face of the heavy claims made upon our malleable natures.

I think my father believed that he could regain, magically, some part of his past,

Armenian refugees load their belongings onto wagons as they flee the Turks.

even alleviate the pain of his exile if he could keep his children Armenian. Thus, he would triumph over the Turk, who had sought to destroy his Armenian identity. So we spoke only Armenian at home, ate only Armenian food, and saw mainly Armenian friends. In those days, the nativist elements used the public schools to disparage the cultural origins of foreigners; I must confess that I was an innocent but willing collaborator. I had no notion that my childish gestures of rebellion might have been torture to my father.

Now I think I know what was eating like acid at my father. Did he deserve the bounty and safety that the New World offered for the earning? Were those signs of success in reality the fruits of his failure as a man? Should he have stayed behind with his parents? Should he have left his sister? Should he have had the courage to confront his enemies, no matter what the cost to him?

I think my father felt guilty that he had escaped the fate of his family. Though he knew that he had avoided terror and even death, in one part of himself he became persuaded that he had betrayed his family by not sharing their destiny, that he had—this will sound irrational to all those but the survivors of concentration camps—survived at their expense.

Thus far his insight took him, no further. The act of sorting out and comprehending these ambivalent feelings proved too much for this uneducated though intelligent immigrant. And indeed why should he have been proud that he had had to run away, even to save his life? This frame of mind was made doubly difficult to endure by obtuse neighbors. . . . He was in America. He was safe. He was prospering. His children had opportunities. What more did he want? Let the dead bury the dead. But my stubborn father could not bring himself to congratulate himself for what he considered to be an act of betrayal.

Fortunately, our society no longer puts pressure on immigrants to forget their former associations, or to deny anything dear left behind. We deplore the bitterness of a destiny that displaces people from their homes, that uproots and deracinates, that creates a league of dislocated persons. Such people are no longer debarred [kept from] from the ranks of "good and true" Americans by virtue of their tragic sense of life. We can be thankful that we have developed this dimension of spiritual tolerance. I prize it and my father, were he alive, would have prized it.

Gene Brown, ed., *Ethnic Groups in American Life.* New York: Arno Press and the *New York Times*, 1978.

CHAPTER TWO

Starting a New Life

America has long had a reputation as the land of opportunity. Until the end of the nineteenth century, the United States owed this reputation in part to its western frontier—a constantly changing line between civilization and the wilderness. Immigrants seeking new opportunities could always go west, beyond the frontier, to areas that had not yet been completely settled by whites (although those who settled on the frontier often encroached on Indian lands). Under the Homestead Act of 1862, land on the Great Plains was free for those willing to farm it and during the 1880s, many immigrants built farms in the Midwest.

By 1890, however, the frontier had all but disappeared. Most of the best land had been settled. For new immigrants, farming was not the clear path to success it had once been. Nevertheless, immigration to the United States continued at record levels. Of the millions of immigrants who came to America between 1900 and 1920, most worked in industry or in jobs requiring craft skills. They tended to settle in the large cities of the Northeast and Midwest.

The massive influx of labor during these years helped the U.S. economy grow at an astounding rate. However, immigrant laborers did not always share in this prosperity. In some of these immigrant cities, particularly New York City, many immigrants lived in run-down apartment buildings known as tenements, where two or more families often crowded together in a single apartment. Then men, women, and even children often labored for long hours under harsh conditions, enduring this life of near poverty in the hopes that their children would fare better than they did.

Other immigrants were able to avoid working in sweatshops or factories. Many of these people came to America not because they were poor, but simply because they had the money and wanted to build a new life in a new country. Although the frontier was gone, America was still a land of opportunity, and many immigrants opened their own shops or other businesses.

Every one of the millions of immigrants who came to the United States faced the challenge of starting a new life in America. The selections in the following chapter detail a few of these experiences.

Advice for Immigrants on Making a Living

In his guidebook for prospective immigrants, S.H. Collins provided a detailed description of all the preparations necessary for the Atlantic voyage to the United States. Collins's guidebook also included warnings about the journey's potential dangers and unscrupulous agents who might take advantage of gullible immigrants. In this excerpt, Collins offers recommendations about finding employment, purchasing land, and traveling inland. He offers different advice for would-be farmers, skilled laborers, and entrepreneurs.

From Europe, until he [the emigrant] arrives [in America], general rules may apply; but now his future destination depends on his choice, and no general rule can be given to direct that choice, because emigrants are of so many different descriptions. In order that these remarks may have a general application, the emigrants shall be considered as consisting of several classes; the remarks shall be applied to each class separately, and terminate with some general observations.

Let us suppose the first to consist of labourers, who have no other trade or profession, and from whose services more is expected to result from bodily strength than from ingenuity or education. If a man of this class will work, he has nothing to fear in the interior of America:—he possesses all the requisites of a farmer, excepting skill; and that he may soon obtain. A great number of farmers have more land inclosed in fence than they can well manage: ask one of these the reason, he replies, "I want help." An assistant enables him to cultivate a portion of his land that would otherwise become overrun with weeds. The emigrant cannot expect full wages in the commencement; but if he be attentive,

Hundreds of immigrants wait to disembark at New York Harbor. Few immigrants knew what to expect in their new homeland.

he may in one year become so expert as to be entitled to what is usually paid to husbandmen,—from twelve to fifteen dollars per month, and board.

But when employment is obtained, the most difficult thing yet remains to be done. . . . If his conduct is proper, he will be allowed to associate with the sons of the neighbouring farmers, many of whom know that their ancestors became proprietors of land from a beginning not more promising than his; even his employer was probably the helper to some one formerly. Before this man can become a complete American farmer, he must learn a number of things not connected with agriculture in some other countries. He must learn to handle the axe dexterously, as he will often be employed to cut down trees. He must also learn, not only to distinguish the different species of trees, but also to know by their appearance whether they will suit the purpose for which they are wanted.

The second class of emigrants to be considered, are those who have trades or professions, and yet are too poor to enter into business for themselves. The primary object of a person of this description is, of course, employment; the commodity he has to dispose of is labour, for which he wants a market. So much of this is daily brought into the sea-ports, by the arrival of emigrants, that they are always overstocked; he must look for a better chance:—this chance the country [farther inland from the port cities] will afford him. If his trade or profession be such as is followed in a city, he may remain two days before he goes to the country; if unsuccessful in his inquiries for work, he ought not to remain longer. During his stay, he ought to inquire amongst those in his own profession, where he may hope to obtain employment; it is very likely they may furnish references which will be very useful to him. In travelling, this man ought not to be sparing in his inquiries; he is not in the least danger of receiving a rude or an uncivil answer, even if he should address himself to a 'squire (so justices are called). It is expected in America, that every man shall attend to his own concerns; and if a man, who is out of work, asks for employment, it is considered as a very natural

thing. He ought to make his situation and profession known at the tavern where he stops, and rather to court than to shun conversation with any that he may find assembled there. He will seldom or never meet with a repulse, as it gives them an opportunity of making inquiries respecting the "old country," (the term usually applied to the British islands). Should he fail in procuring employment at his own business, he has all the advantages of the first man in agriculture. . . .

The man possessed of some property, say from 200 pounds to 1000 pounds, has more need of cautionary advice than either of the former. But no knowledge can be conveyed to him that will be so valuable as what results from his own experience and observations. He is advised to deposit his money in a bank, or vest it in government stock, immediately on landing and for which he will receive interest seven percent. His next object is to determine in what line of life he shall employ himself and his capital. In this he should avoid being too hasty. If it is known that he has money, he will probably be tempted to enter into speculations, both by his own countrymen and others. Designing men are much more likely to hold out such temptations, than men with honest and honourable intentions; and, until he has acquired a competent knowledge of men and things, it is dangerous for him to embark in business. . . . He ought, if possible, to take with him letters of introduction to some persons in the United States, experienced in matters of business, whom he might occasionally consult. If he decide on mercantile business, or keeping a store, he ought by all means to procure a situation in a merchant's counting-house, or in a store, for one year at least, even if with only trifling [small] wages, he will still be a gainer. If he adopt agriculture, he ought to obtain, if possible, an assistant, who knows the management of crops, and the mode of working the ground; such a person will be necessary at least for two years. If he should not succeed in procuring such a man, he must keep on good terms with his neighbours, who will cheerfully tell him what is necessary to be done. In purchasing his land, he ought not to depend entirely on his own judgment, unless he has made an extensive tour through the country, and attentively considered the subject of land.

S.H. Collins, *The Emigrant's Guide to and Description of the United States.* Hull, J. Noble, 1830.

Struggling to Make Ends Meet

The immigration experience always entailed risks, and many immigrants found that their life in America was not what they expected. In the selection below, Della Adler recounts how her grandfather came to the United States from Lithuania. She explains that he was robbed during his journey and lived in poverty for three years before his situation improved.

Grandfather—Jacob H. Mayerberg—came to this country in 1867, from a small place in Lithuania called Volkovisk. His original mission was a business one, and he expected to return [to Lithuania]. Destiny decided otherwise.

He had heard that the U.S.A., especially New York City, was perishing from a need for *seforim*—Hebrew books of learning. So, the idea was to come here with a stock of books, sell them at a good profit, and return.

Poor Grandfather! On the way over, every book—plus all else he possessed— was stolen, and he arrived . . . destitute.

He did what he was totally unequipped for—physically and by nature—he peddled. What with, I do not know, but I do know he peddled through New York State in deep, drifted snow and icy winds and finally reached Buffalo and settled down as a *melamed*, a Hebrew teacher. The late Willard Saperston was one of his *talmidim*, his students. He thus eked out a pathetic living in bleak, dreary surroundings, and there Grandmother Hennie and their four children found him when they arrived in this country some three years later.

Grandma's comment on first seeing him was, "Yankov [Jacob] Hirsch, what happened to you? In three years you have become an old man." He was then forty-seven years old.

Grandmother was not one just to sit and do nothing. Her first effort was to find respectable living quarters. To pay the rent, she sold her most valuable possession, six silver spoons. The day came when there was no money to pay another month's rent, and Yankov Hirsch and Hennie assumed a "the Lord will provide" attitude; and the Lord, blessed be He, did provide.

Came a knock on their door, one fine day. A man of friendly mien [demeanor] stood there and asked—did they have one large or two small rooms to rent to six men who peddled in the country and came home just for *Shabbos* [the Sabbath]? There were five married men whose wives were [waiting] . . . to come to America, and there was one twenty-one-year-old unmarried youngster who was being petted and spoiled by the older men. Each Thursday, one of the six came home to cook for *Shabbos*. The other five came home on Friday.

The Mayerbergs could, and did, rent them rooms, and this miraculously solved the rent problem for them, until they could scramble to their feet. The single man, Louis Rubenstein, married the eldest daughter of the Mayerbergs, Kate—Chayeh—and they became my parents.

This all happened in the very long ago. Both the Mayerbergs and my parents prospered in a very modest way, and thereafter needed no crutch.

Today, I am the last living member of the Louis Rubenstein family, and the memory of the six silver spoons still lingers.

Abraham J. Karp, ed., *Golden Door to America: The Jewish Immigrant Experience*. New York: Viking, 1976.

The Life of a Homesteader

Settlers who took advantage of the 1862 Homestead Act, which granted free land in the Great Plains to those willing to farm it, were called homesteaders. Many homesteaders were immigrants, and most of these immigrants were from Europe. In the account below, Austrian American Joe Poeffel recounts how his father established their homestead in Nebraska in 1877.

We had a small farm near Deutchausen, in Austria, and when I was about ten years old I had to help with the farm work, herd cattle, haul wood out of the timber. We farmed with oxen those days, and when there was a lot of field work to do we used to hitch up a cow with them but it was slow work. We did not raise very much small grain and we did our threshing with a "flail", which is a long stick with another stick or club fastened on the end, the grain was loose and was laid on boards and with the flail we pounded out the grain.

My father was anxious to come to America, but he did not want to take my mother or any of us along, saying that it would be too wild a country and that there were too many Indians here that we might get killed.

He then started out alone to this country in 1877, he worked as a hired farm hand and also did some carpenter work around, and bought a homestead from another man, paying $1.00 an acre for it and he proved up on it. He then sent for us in 1879, my mother, one brother and two sisters. . . . I remember my father met us at the train with a pair of oxen hitched to a lumber wagon and we kids sat on a board in the wagon box, and it took us a long time to get home. . . .

We lived in three different sod houses for about ten years. The first one was near a creek and one time a big rain storm

Homesteaders pose for a photographer. During the late nineteenth century, many immigrants became homesteaders, taking advantage of the government's offer of free land.

came up and the water got so high that it came through the door and windows of our sod house, the furniture that we had was swimming around in the house; we had to run to the granary and there was high water on both sides of it so we could not get out and had to stay there until the water went down the next afternoon. We lost a lot of chickens and sixteen head of hogs that weighed 200 pounds a piece. The water had ruined our sod house so that it caved in the next day and then we had to build a new one, which we made of square blocks of prairie laid together like our cement blocks are now and smoothed on the inside with mortar that was made of sticky mud, we would whitewash the inside walls to make it look nice; it was

warm in the house in winter time and pretty cool in the summer time.

When I was still at home we did not have much money, we would make our own coffee by roasting barley in the oven; we used this kind of coffee for about ten years. Coffee cost about sixty cents a pound and when we used it, it would be as a special treat on Sundays.

I herded cattle away from home for two summers for which I was paid $18 for the season; worked as a hired man on the farm for three years and helped at home until I was twenty-nine years old when I got married. Then got 80 acres of land from my father and started farming for myself.

In the year of 1880, about the middle of October, we had one of the worst blizzards that I remember of, it lasted for three days and three nights. I was working out at that time; our barn was just about under, we had to start shoveling snow on the roof so that we could get into the barn to milk the cows. We would have to hitch four mules to the hayrack to get half a load of hay for the cattle. We had a blizzard about three times a week that winter and it got to 35 below zero.

The next spring about the middle of April, when the wheat and oats were all sowed, we had another three day blizzard and everything froze. It was one of the coldest winters I ever went through.

Library of Congress, *American Life Stories: Manuscripts from the Federal Writers' Project, 1936–1940* American Memory website. http://memory.loc.gov/ammem/wpaintro/wpahome.html.

Life in the Tenements

From the nineteenth century to the early twentieth century, three-quarters of all immigrants entered the United States by way of New York City, and many of them settled there permanently. They were immediately confronted by the need to find housing, a challenge in the overcrowded city, and many immigrants ended up in rundown apartment buildings called tenements. In the following excerpts, writer Jacob Riis describes the overcrowding and poverty in New York City tenements. Riis, an immigrant himself, was a photojournalist who campaigned on behalf of the foreign-born poor throughout his career.

In a Stanton Street tenement, the other day, I stumbled upon a Polish capmaker's home. There were other capmakers in the house, Russian and Polish, but they simply "lived" there. This one had a home. The fact proclaimed itself the moment the door was opened, in spite of the darkness. The rooms were in the rear, gloomy with the twilight of the tenement, although the day was sunny . . . but neat, even cosy. It was early, but the day's chores were evidently done. The teakettle sang on the stove, at which a bright-looking girl of twelve, with a pale but cheery face, and sleeves brushed back to the elbows, was busy poking up the fire. A little boy stood by the window, flattening his nose against the pane and gazing wistfully up among the chimney pots where a piece of blue sky about as big as the kitchen could be made out. I remarked to the mother that they were nice rooms.

"Ah yes," she said, with a weary little smile that struggled bravely with hope long deferred, "but it is hard to make a home here. We would so like to live in the front, but we can't pay the rent."

I knew the front with its unlovely view of the tenement street too well, and I said a good word for the air shaft—yard or court it could not be called, it was too small for that—which rather surprised myself. I had found few virtues enough in it before. The girl at the stove had left off poking the fire. She broke in the moment I finished, with eager enthusiasm: "Why, they have the sun in there. When the door is opened the light comes right in your face."

"Does it never come here?" I asked, and wished I had not done so, as soon as the words were spoken. The child at the window

For many immigrants who settled in New York City, overcrowded, run-down tenements like this one became home.

was listening, with his whole hungry little soul in his eyes.

"Yes, it did," she said. Once every summer, for a little while, it came over the houses. She knew the month and the exact hour of the day when its rays shone into their home, and just the reach of its slant on the wall. They had lived there six years. In June the sun was due. A haunting fear that the baby would ask how long it was till June—it was February then—took possession of me, and I hastened to change the subject. . . .

The capmaker's case is the case of the nineteenth century, of civilization, against the metropolis of America. The home, the family, are the rallying points of civilization. But long since the tenements of New York earned for it the ominous name of "the homeless city." In its 40,000 tenements its workers, more than half of the city's population, are housed. They have no other chance. There are, indeed, wives and mothers who, by sheer force of character, rise above their environment and make homes where they go. Happily, there are yet many of them. But the fact remains that hitherto their struggle has been growing ever harder, and the issue more doubtful.

The tenement itself, with its crowds, its lack of privacy, is the greatest destroyer of individuality, of character. As its numbers increase, so does "the element that becomes criminal for lack of individuality and the self-respect that comes with it." Add the shiftless and the weak who are turned out by the same process, and you have its legitimate crop. In 1880 the average number of persons to each dwelling in New York was 16.37; in 1890 it was 18.52. In 1895, according to the police census, 21.2. The census of 1900 will show the crowding to have gone on at an equal if not at a greater rate. That will mean that so many more tenements have been built of the modern type, with four families to the floor where once there were two. . . .

It is no answer to the charge that New York's way of housing its workers is the worst in the world to say that they are better off than they were where they came from. It is not true, in most cases, as far as the home is concerned: a shanty is better than a flat in a cheap tenement, any day. Even if it were true, it would still be beside the issue. In Poland my capmaker counted for nothing. Nothing was expected of him. Here he ranks, after a few brief years, politically equal with the man who hires his labor. A citizen's duty is expected of him, and home and citizenship are convertible terms. . . .

Suppose we take a stroll through a tenement-house neighborhood and see for ourselves. We were in Stanton Street. Let us start there, then, going east. Towering barracks on either side, five, six stories high. Teeming crowds. Push-cart men "moved on" by the policeman, who seems to exist only for the purpose. . . .

Here is a block of tenements inhabited by poor Jews. Most of the Jews who live over here are poor; and the poorer they are, the higher rent do they pay, and the more do they crowd to make it up between them. "The destruction of the poor is their poverty." It is only the old story in a new setting. The slum landlord's profits were always the highest. He spends nothing for repairs, and lays the blame on the tenant. . . .

A more unlovely existence than that in one of these tenements it would be hard to imagine. Everywhere is the stench of the kerosene stove that is forever burning, serving for cooking, heating, and ironing alike, until the last atom of oxygen is burned out of the close air. . . . The stuffy rooms seem as if they were made for dwarfs. Most decidedly, there is not room to swing the proverbial cat in any one of them. . . .

High rents, slack work, and low wages go hand in hand in the tenements as promoters of overcrowding. The rent is always one fourth of the family income, often more. The fierce competition for a bare living cuts down wages; and when loss of work is added, the only thing left is to take in lodgers to meet the landlord's claim.

Jacob Riis, *A Ten Years' War: An Account of the Battle with the Slum in New York*. Freeport, NY: Books for Libraries Press, 1969.

A Description of Working-Class Life

Industrial workers often had to relocate to various towns throughout the country in order to obtain work and make ends meet. Here, Joe Rudiak, who grew up in a Polish family, documents the realities of living in Lyndora, Pennsylvania, during the early twentieth century. Rubiak describes the immigrant community in Lyndora as being separate from the rest of the town and explains how the community served as a stopover point for migrant workers.

My father came from Poland in 1900 and began working as a miner near Berwick, Pennsylvania. Then we moved to Lyndora, near Butler, where he worked for Standard Steel Car Company. He did physical labor, very hard work. It was building freight cars, fabricating freight cars. He worked in the paint shop. He painted cars, and did odd jobs, mostly in the paint department.

We lived in company houses owned by the Standard Steel Company, and each one of these—we'll say it was six apartments—were all frame and painted red. And at that time there was a shortage of housing because there was a need for labor, hard physical labor, and there was [many laborers,] all mostly from the Eastern part of Europe—the Poles, Slovaks, Yugoslavs, the Serbian people. [This labor force] even touched the Middle East. It was a ghetto. They had, lined up for let's say about half a mile and about five hundred feet deep,

rows of these shanties. We called it shanties. As high as five, six, seven boarders would come in. They had to find places for 'em. So here they'd come in from their hometown; one pulled the other in, for instance, to house him until they'd be able to find something. . . .

It was sort of a stopover point. They would work in the car shop; some of 'em could take it; some of 'em couldn't take it. And they were seeking other accommodations as far as rooms and better working conditions [were concerned]. And they would scatter some. This was more of a stopover point for 'em. They didn't know it, but the first thing you know, the man would leave, and he would be in Chicago or working in a steel mill in Cleveland or Detroit. Detroit was [getting] active then as far as the automobile industry was concerned. And they were mostly moving from one city to the next, more or less like migrant labor. And that was it. So then another one would move in until finally the Depression came along. And there was no such thing as boarders at that time.

They had a public school. The Standard Steel people that lived in these particular shanties went to the Butler public schools. And the people that lived across the street that belonged to the township, they went to the township schools. And there was no such thing as parochial schools. They did not provide much as far as schooling was concerned.

I would say the population living in Lyndora and the shanties right across the street—made up of all the ethnics, a few

Germans, a few Italians, no Irish, and no English—was about three thousand including the children.

It was very rare that anybody from that section of Butler, or that suburb of Butler, up to 1925, would graduate from high school. I would say in that period of time up to about 1929 that about eighth grade, elementary school, was normal for a person to stop going to school.

The children would work or they would be unemployed and leave town to seek other employment, such as [in] Detroit, which was becoming very popular with the automobile industry.

I quit high school because I became sick and [then I] went to work. My oldest brother was sort of crippled. I don't think he went to work till he was about seventeen or eighteen years of age, that's the oldest brother. The next-to-the-oldest brother went to work about nine years of age, in the glassworks. There was also glass plants where they employed child labor and all that. So my brother was about nine years old, and it was quite common. . . .

Shanty houses like this one provided temporary homes for migrating workers.

And of the things my mother insisted on, education (as far as elementary school was concerned or high school) was one of them. Mother insisted, with a few other families, at least to educate us [in] our own native tongue and [in] writing [at the] language schools. They formed language schools through the churches. And that was a must with most families. That was a must. I don't know why they did it. I guess it was on account of their background, [their] loneliness and everything for their own countries. . . .

We didn't join American organizations though. There was no drive on among the nationality people, no drive on by the politicians. You've got to understand that they didn't want these people to vote in the first place. The companies controlled the towns. They controlled the courthouse. They controlled the police. They controlled the state police, the coal mine police. There was no encouragement for people to vote up until the Depression. I would say [that] even then, among the immigrants, every one of them that came into this country had the feeling that they were going back. And once they would take their citizenship here, they were breaking up their ties with their home countries. That was a cruel thing, that they were never able to get enough money to do it. And they were still communicating with many people in their home country. You know, they'd have people coming in a year later, two years later, and they'd say, "Well, how's things there? Are they better? Nothing new? No? Well, that's the reason I'm here."

Quoted in *The Immigrant Experience: History in Your Hands*. CD-ROM. Primary Source Media, 1996.

The Plight of a Chinese Laundryman

Because of widespread discrimination, Chinese immigrants during the early part of the twentieth century were usually denied jobs in agriculture or manufacturing. As a result, service occupations such as restaurant and laundry work were the only ways that many Chinese immigrants could make a living. In the following selection, a laundryman discusses the life he has chosen and the sacrifices he has made to ensure the welfare of his children. Laundry work, he points out, takes a heavy toll on his health, and his only hope lies in his children's future.

Being a laundryman is no life at all. I work fourteen hours a day and I have to send home [to China] almost all my wages. You see, I have a big family at home. My mother is still living and I have an unmarried sister who is going to school. My own children, five of them, all are in school too. My brother here—he is no help; he has a family here and what he earns is just enough to support his family. I figure I send home about fifteen hundred dollars a year, at least, sometimes more.

I seldom go down to Chinatown. . . . Unless I have some business matter, I usually go to Chinatown only once a month. I sleep and read here Sunday. I don't go to movies

People think I am a happy person. I am not. I worry very much. First, I don't like this kind of life; it is not human life. To be a laundryman is to be just a slave. I work because I have to. If I ever stop working, those at home must stop eating.

I am not healthy at all. I feel my backaches all the time. My health has improved however since my tonsils were removed. Then I have other troubles, like headaches. I am not an old man yet, but I feel old. How can a man feel good when he is forced into an occupation he doesn't like?

But I get used to it. After you are on it for so many years, you have no more feeling but stay on with it. After all, you can't get rich but you don't have to worry about money as long as you can work. If my father had let me stay in school, I could have graduated from middle school; then I might not have come [to America]. I could find something to do in China. It is better to be a poor teacher in China. You could have been happier.

In this country, one must know English enough to do something other than laundry work. I was not allowed to have a chance

A man parcels clothes in a laundry shop, one of the few jobs open to Chinese immigrants.

often. You don't understand a lot of the things they say in the show. Sometimes I get tired and fall asleep in the movie theater.

I buy lottery tickets but do not patronize any other Chinatown gambling. I used to play ma-jong [a popular Chinese game] when I was in Canton [China]. I do not have the energy to enjoy playing it any more. . . . I have never had any luck.

to study English when I first came here. My father and uncles had an idea that those who knew enough English were those who could become bad. He meant, to fool around with girls and so forth. I was foolish to listen to them though. Think of that sort of old ideas! How stupid!

I have a building in Canton. It cost my father about nine thousand dollars. My family is now living on one of the four floors; the other floors are rented. It is lucky we don't have to pay rent, otherwise my responsibility could be heavier. That was all my father left us.

Paul C.P. Siu, "The Old-Timer," in *The Chinese Laundryman: A Study of Social Isolation*. Ed. by John Kuo Wei Tchen. New York: New York University Press, 1987.

A Fortunate Filipino American

The following selection is Emigdio Cabico's account of his immigration to the Hawaiian Islands in 1926. Unlike most Filipino immigrants, who worked long hours in the Hawaiian sugarcane fields, Cabico was offered a job at a plantation store because of his ability to speak and write English.

There is one agent, sent by the Hawaiian Sugar Planters' Association, to recruit labor for Hawaii. He explain to us about Hawaii. He says it's good to come. The agent promise us if we stay here for three years, we have free passage to go back home. Then if we wanted to come back again, all us can come back to Hawaii free passage. See, free. Yeah, that's what they promise us. Of course, when we reach Hawaii, he said we would have free house and everything, you know. And, the work contract is eighteen dollars a month. So, naturally, we, young boys, was listening him one time. We told him we are interested to come to Hawaii. I wanted to come to continue my studies and earn money, particularly to help my parents. . . .

I arrived here in Hawaii, that was January 1926. About sixty-five people arrived here in Waialua; most of us does not know how to speak English and write. Naturally, the clerks . . . could hardly spell our names. So, they ask us who can write and spell. Since I attended up to three months in the fifth grade, I raise my hand. I write all the names, and when they see that my handwriting is so nice, they thought I'm a well-educated man. That's what happened. (Laughs) Then they assign us to Kawailoa, but they told me don't work on that day, because they wanted to talk to me.

So, that morning, I didn't show up to work and the policeman came to my house and told me, "Eh, boy, you going jail!"

I say, "Why?"

"You go in the plantation office because the manager want to see you."

I say, "Oh, okay." We went to the office and the manager ask me what kind of job I wanted. I said, "I'm not so choosy. Any kind."

"Do you want to work in the hospital? Work in the office? Or work in the store?"

"Well, I prefer to work in the store, if

you give me a chance."

He said, "Well, you take the test. If you pass the test, then you are qualified to work in the store."

So that day, we are about eight to take the test. They give us pencil, tablet; all the test was written in the blackboard. Within thirty or thirty-five minute, I would say, I finish. It was so simple. . . .

So, from the next day, they took me to the plantation store. That's how I get my job as a clerk.

From the beginning I work in the store so I didn't work hard. But others work in the field, eh, and whenever they come home from work, I see them. They are so tired; their job is so hard. Maybe, I'm very fortunate that I never work in the field.

Emigdio Cabico, "Lucky I Never Work Field," in Michi Kodama-Nishimoto, Warren S. Nishimoo, and Cynthia A. Oshiro, eds., *Hanahana: An Oral History of Hawaii's Working People*. Manoa, HI: Center for Oral History: University of Hawaii, 1984.

CHAPTER THREE

Struggling with Assimilation and Discrimination

America is famous for its "melting pot" of cultures, meaning that the United States is a country populated by people who blend many different kinds of traditions. But this phrase is somewhat misleading, since it implies that immigrants to the United States were easily able to adapt and contribute to mainstream American culture. This, however, was not at all the case for millions of immigrants who helped to shape the nation's multicultural society. Many immigrants had difficulty reconciling their traditional culture with that of their new homeland. Others experienced discrimination, hostility, and violence because their culture was different from that of the people who had come before them.

During the nineteenth century, when non-English immigrants first began coming to the United States in large numbers, each new group experienced some degree of discrimination. The Irish immigrants who arrived during the 1840s provoked anti-immigrant sentiments because they were largely Catholic, whereas most Americans were Protestant. German immigrants who arrived during the same period were attacked because many of them tried to hang on to their native language rather than learn English. After the Civil War, the influx of Asian, southern and eastern European, and Jewish immigrants spurred increasingly strong calls to restrict immigration.

The Chinese, however, were the first group on which such restrictions were placed. In general, anti-immigrant protest during the late nineteenth and early twentieth centuries was most strongly directed against Asians. Many white Americans believed that the Chinese immigrants on the West Coast were too "different" to ever become true Americans (white Americans also didn't want to compete with Chinese immigrants for work). As a result, in 1882, Congress passed the Chinese Exclusion Act, which prohibited almost all further Chinese immigration. In 1907, similar sentiments prompted the U.S. government to establish the "Gentleman's Agreement" with Japan, a law under which the Japanese government agreed to prohibit Japanese emigration to the United States. These restrictions were not lifted until well into the twentieth century.

In the face of the pressure to assimilate and become "true" Americans, many immigrants choose to adopt mainstream American values and traditions. Others, who retain their native language and culture, find that their children (often called second-generation immigrants) naturally absorb the culture of the country where they are raised. Many immigrants are ambivalent about this process. Most are proud to be Americans but they are also proud of their native cultures and are often disappointed when their children do not carry on those cultures. Furthermore, in immigrant families that have fully assimilated into mainstream American culture, some second-, third-, and later-generation immigrants may feel deprived of their heritage.

Although discrimination against people who are different certainly still exists, Americans today are, in general, a more tolerant people than they were in the past. This atmosphere has encouraged more immigrants and their descendants to embrace both their native heritage and their identity as Americans. The selections in this chapter explore the tensions immigrants experience as a result of cultural differences and how some immigrants have handled them.

The Chinese Exclusion Act

In 1882 the Chinese became the first group to be forbidden to immigrate to the United States. Large groups of Chinese immigrants first began arriving in America in 1853 in response to the California gold rush. After the Civil War, they competed with white Californians for jobs in mining, construction, agriculture, and manufacturing. Anti-Chinese bias led to frequent violence by white workers against the Chinese, and in 1882 Congress passed the Chinese Exclusion Act. The act, excerpted below, forbade further Chinese immigration, made it a crime to bring Chinese immigrants to the United States, and denied citizenship to Chinese immigrants who had already arrived in America.

Whereas, In the opinion of the Government of the United States, the coming of Chinese laborers to this country endangers the good order of certain localities within the territory thereof: Therefore,

During the late nineteenth century, Chinese immigrants became victims of violence and discrimination.

Be it enacted by the Senate and House of Representatives of the United States of America in Congress assembled, That from and after the expiration of ninety days next after the passage of this Act, and until the expiration of ten years next after the passage of this Act, the coming of Chinese laborers to the United States be, and the same is hereby, suspended; and during such suspension it shall not be lawful for any Chinese laborer to come, or, having so come after the expiration of said ninety days, to remain within the United States. . . .

SECTION 2. That the master of any vessel who shall knowingly bring within the United States on such vessel, and land or permit to be landed, any Chinese laborer, from any foreign port or place, shall be deemed guilty of a misdemeanor, and on conviction thereof shall be punished by a fine of not more than five hundred dollars for each and every such Chinese laborer so brought, and may be also imprisoned for a term not exceeding one year. . . .

SECTION 11. That any person who shall knowingly bring into or cause to be brought into the United States by land, or who shall knowingly aid or abet the same, or aid or abet the landing in the United States from any vessel of any Chinese person not lawfully entitled to enter the United States, shall be deemed guilty of a misdemeanor, and shall, on conviction thereof, be fined in a sum not exceeding one thousand dollars, and imprisoned for a term not exceeding one year. . . .

SECTION 12. That no Chinese person shall be permitted to enter the United States by land without producing to the proper officer of customs, the certificate in this act required of Chinese persons seeking to land from a vessel. And any Chinese person found unlawfully within the United States shall be caused to be removed therefrom to the country from whence he came, by direction of the President of the United States, and at the cost of the United States, after being brought before some justice, judge, or commissioner of a Court of the United States and found to be one not lawfully entitled to remain in the United States. . . .

SECTION 14. That hereafter no State Court or Court of the United States shall admit Chinese to citizenship; and all laws in conflict with this Act are hereby repealed.

Chinese Exclusion Act, 1882.

The Forces of Assimilation

In an 1890 text, social scientist Richmond Mayo-Smith recognized that economics and politics both exert a strong assimilating influence on immigrants. According to Mayo-Smith, economic prosperity causes an immigrant to identify more with America than with his old country, a feeling that increases with later generations until the immigrants' descendants are completely Americanized. Mayo-Smith also writes that new citizens come to identify with the American political system by exercising their right to vote.

There are, fortunately, certain forces which tend to counteract [the] exclusiveness on the part of immigrants and gradually to fuse the different elements into one American nationality. [These are] economic prosperity and the practice of free political institutions. The former widens the circle of wants of the new citizen and leads him to imitate the higher style of living which he sees about him. This separates him from the habits and traditions of his native country and he adopts new standards which are associated in his mind with the new domicile, and which produce a feeling of superiority when he revisits the old home or comes into contact with later arrivals. It differentiates him, so to speak, from the immigrant, and gives him a feeling of attachment to the country where he has prospered. This feeling increases with his children and grandchildren until they become fully identified with our customs, manner of living and habits of thought, and are thoroughly Americanized.

The exercise of political rights, to which many of the immigrants are strange, tends to differentiate them in much the same way. It makes them of importance to the political leaders. It gives them a higher position than they were accustomed to at home, and this naturally attaches them to the new country. However much our politics may suffer from the addition of this vote, much of it ignorant and some of it depraved, there is no doubt as to the educational and nationalizing effect of the suffrage on the immigrants themselves. However attached the Irishman may be to the cause of home rule for Ireland, or however proud the German may be of the military glory of the empire, his feelings must gradually and unconsciously gravitate to the country where he has found economic prosperity and political recognition. He may still observe the national feast days and wave the old flag, but if it ever came to a contest, he would probably find that he was more of an American than an Irishman or German.

Richmond Mayo-Smith, *Emigration and Immigration: A Study in Social Science*. New York: Scribner's Sons, 1890.

Multiculturalism and Tolerance in a New York City Public School

The millions of immigrants who came to the United States after 1880 turned many American cities into immigrant cities, populated with residents from all over the world. Although racism and discrimination were certainly problems for immigrants in these cities, tolerance for different ethnic groups was often higher in the eastern port cities than in other areas where people were not exposed to other cultures. In the following account, journalist A.R. Dugmore claims that at a New York City high school he investigated, children from different backgrounds got along well.

At the corner of Catharine and Henry Streets in New York is a large white building that overlooks and dominates its neighborhood. Placed in the middle of a region of tawdry flathouses and dirty streets, it

School children salute the American flag in New York, where tolerance for different ethnic groups was often higher than in other cities.

stands out preëminent because of its solid cleanliness and unpretentiousness. It is the home of Public School No. 1. In it are centred all the hopes of the miserably poor polyglot [multilingual] population of the surrounding district—for its pupils the scene of their greatest interest and endeavor, and for their parents an earnest of the freedom they have come far and worked hard to attain.

The child of American parentage is the exception in this school. The pupils are of the different nationalities or races that have their separate quarters in the immediate neighborhood. If they were to be divided according to their parental nationality,

there would be twenty-five or more groups. The majority of the pupils, however, are Swedes, Austrians, Greeks, Russians, English, Irish, Scotch, Welsh, Rumanians, Italians, Poles, Hungarians, Canadians, Armenians, Germans and Chinese. The Germans, Russians and Polish predominate [dominate], for there are a very large number of Jewish pupils.

The most noticeable thing in the school is the perfectly friendly equality in which all these races mix; no prejudice is noticeable. The different races are so scattered that there is no chance for organization and its attendant cliques and small school politics. This is particularly interesting in the face of the fact that the one thing more than any other which binds the boys together is their intense common interest in party and city politics. All political news is followed and every question is heatedly debated in and out of class. This interest in politics and the training in argument and oratory it brings is probably due in large measure to the parents. To them this opportunity for political discussion is an evidence of the freedom of the new country which has replaced the tyranny of the old. The lack of organization and the lack of prejudice is shown by the fact that the "captain" or elected leader of a class composed with one exception of Jewish lads is the solitary exception—an Irish boy. In another class the "captain" is Chinese.

A.R. Dugmore, "New Citizens of the Republic," *World's Week*, April 1903.

Struggling with an Unfamiliar Language

Whether in the cities or in rural areas, immigrants often lived close to one another in large enclaves, where they spoke the language of their native country and practiced their native traditions. However, not all immigrants were comfortable within these communities. In the following 1914 letter to a Boston newspaper, a Polish immigrant writes of his struggle to learn English and find a well-paying job.

I am polish man. I want be american citizen. . . . But my friends are polish people—I must live with them—I work in the shoes-shop with polish people—I stay all the time with them—at home—in the shop—anywhere.

I want live with american people, but I do not know anybody of american. I go 4 times to teacher and must pay $2 weekly. I wanted take board in english house, but I could not, for I earn only $5 or 6 in a week, and when I pay teacher $2, I have only $4—$3—and now english board house is too dear for me. Better job to get is very hard for me, because I do not speak well english and I cannot understand what they say to me. The teacher teach me—but when I come home—I must speak polish and in the shop also. In this way I can live in your country many years—like my friends—and never speak—write well english—and never be good american citizen. I know here many persons, they live here 10 or moore years, and they are not citizens, they don't speak well english, they don't know geography and history of this country, they don't know constitution of America—nothing. I don't like be like them I wanted they help me in english—they could not—because they knew nothing. I want go from them away. But where? Not in the country, because I want go in the city, free evening schools and lern. I'm looking for help. If somebody could give me another job between american people, help me live with them and lern english—and could tell me the best way how I can fast lern—it would be very, very good for me. Perhaps you have somebody, here he could help me?

If you can help me, I please you.

I wrote this letter by myself and I know

no good—but I hope you will understand whate I mean.

"Letter of an Anonymous Polish Immigrant to the Massachusetts Commission on Immigration, August 1914," Report of the Commission on the Problem of Immigration in Massachusetts, Boston, 1914.

 ## Racism Feeds Anti-Immigrant Views

By the early 1900s anti-immigrant sentiment had become fairly widespread among native Americans (during this period, the term "native Americans" did not refer to American Indians, but was instead sometimes used to describe whites whose ancestors had arrived one or more generations ago). This feeling, called "nativism," was often based on blatantly racist ideas. In this excerpt from his 1916 book The Passing of the Great Race, *author Madison Grant writes that native Americans have traditionally come from northern and western Europe, and that immigrants from other areas of the world threaten to corrupt America's genetic stock.*

The native American by the middle of the nineteenth century was rapidly becoming a distinct type. Derived from the Teutonic part of the British Isles, and being almost purely Nordic, he was on the point of developing physical peculiarities of his own, slightly variant from those of his English forefathers, and corresponding rather with the idealistic Elizabethan than with the materialistic Hanoverian Englishman. The Civil War, however, put a severe, perhaps fatal, check to the development and expansion of this splendid type, by destroying great numbers of the best breeding stock on both sides, and by breaking up the home ties of many more. If the war had not occurred these same men with their descendants would have populated the Western States instead of the racial nondescripts who are now flocking there.

The prosperity that followed the war attracted hordes of newcomers who were welcomed by the native Americans to operate factories, build railroads, and fill up the waste spaces—"developing the country" it was called.

These new immigrants were no longer exclusively members of the Nordic race as were the earlier ones who came of their own impulse to improve their social conditions. The transportation lines advertised America as a land flowing with milk and honey, and the European governments took the opportunity to unload upon careless, wealthy, and hospitable America the sweepings of their jails and asylums. The result was that the new immigration, while it still included many strong elements from the north of Europe, contained a large and increasing number of the weak, the broken, and the mentally crippled of all races drawn from the lowest stratum of the Mediterranean basin and the Balkans, together with hordes of the wretched, submerged populations of the Polish Ghettos.

With a pathetic and fatuous [silly] belief in the efficacy [effectiveness] of American institutions and environment to reverse or obliterate immemorial [extending back beyond memory] hereditary tendencies, these newcomers were welcomed and given a share in our land and prosperity. The American taxed himself to sanitate and educate these poor helots [serfs or slaves], and as soon as they could speak English, encouraged them to enter into the political life, first of municipalities, and then of the nation.

The result is showing plainly in the rapid decline in the birth rate of native Americans because the poorer classes of Colonial stock, where they still exist, will not bring children into the world to compete in the labor market with the Slovak, the Italian, the Syrian, and the Jew. The native American is too proud to mix socially with them, and is gradually withdrawing from the scene, abandoning to these aliens the land which he conquered and developed. The man of the old stock is being crowded out of many country districts by these foreigners, just as he is to-day being literally driven off the streets of New York City by the swarms of Polish Jews. These immigrants adopt the language of the native American; they wear his clothes; they steal his name; and they are beginning to take his women, but they seldom adopt his religion or understand his ideals, and while he is being elbowed out of his own home the American looks calmly abroad and urges on others the suicidal ethics which are exterminating his own race.

Madison Grant, *The Passing of the Great Race*. New York: Charles Scribner's Sons, 1916.

The End of the Era of Open Immigration

During the 1920s, anti-immigrant sentiment in the United States led Congress to pass a series of laws that ended the era of open immigration. These laws instituted a quota system, known as the National Origins System, that governed the number of immigrants that would be allowed annually from specific countries. This quota system favored immigrants from northern and western Europe. Congressman William Vaile defended the National Origins System with the following remarks.

We would not want any immigrants at all unless we could hope that they would become assimilated to our language, customs, and institutions, unless they could blend thoroughly into our body politic. This would be admitted, I suppose, by the most radical opponent of immigration restriction. In fact, it is one of the stock arguments of these gentlemen that, although the immigrant himself may be assimilated slowly, his children, born here, become Americans in thought, action, speech, and character. That statement, often splendidly true, must nevertheless be accepted with many qualifications; but at least it is clear enough that the second generation will be assimilated quicker than the first—whatever may be the effect in many cases of such assimilation upon the United States. It would seem still clearer that the third and subsequent generations will be still more American than their predecessors.

It is also one of the stock arguments of the antirestrictionists that the immigrant has taken an important part in the building up of the country. Surely his children and grandchildren, both in numbers and in the quality of their work, have taken a still more important part.

Now, it seems rather illogical for gentlemen who vaunt [boast] the assimilability and the work of alien groups in our population to claim that those who have been for the shortest time in the process of assimilation and in the work of the Republic should have greater or even equal consideration because of this very newness. It would seem if those who came to the work at the eleventh hour are to have a penny, then at least those who have "borne the heat and burden of the day" should not be put off with a farthing [something of small value].

It is a fact, not merely an argument, that this country was created, kept united, and developed—at least for more than a century of existence—almost entirely by people who came here from the countries of northern and western Europe. That people from southern and eastern Europe did not begin to come in large numbers until after 1890 certainly proves that those who came before them had built up a country desirable enough to attract these late comers.

Shall the countries which furnished those earlier arrivals be discriminated against for the very reason . . . that they are represented here by from 2 to 10 generations of American citizens, whereas the others are largely represented by people who have not been here long enough to become citizens at all?

If there is a charge of "discrimination," the charge necessarily involves the idea that the proposed quota varies from some standard which is supposed to be not "discriminatory." What is that standard? From the arguments of those opposed to the bill it would appear that the census of 1910 is now regarded as not "discriminatory," or at least as less "discriminatory" than the census of 1890. It will be remembered that the census of 1910 was adopted as a base for emergency legislation, legislation not expected to be permanent, legislation not claimed to be exact, but intended to answer the purpose of an urgently needed restriction of the total volume of immigration. It has answered that purpose fairly well, but with some unnecessary hardships obviated [eliminated] by the present bill. The number admitted under it, however, has been far too great, and it is now proposed to cut the quota more than one-half.

But it is not the cut in the total which is so bitterly complained of. It is the change in the proportions, and it is interesting to note that those who violently opposed the passage of the 3 per cent law now with equal violence demand the retention of its proportions in the present legislation. But at least we can say that it has not been in operation long enough to have become an established and inviolable principle of distribution if some more equitable basis could be devised.

Moses Rischin, ed., *Immigration and the American Tradition*. Indianapolis: Bobbs-Merrill, 1976.

A Plea to Lift Immigration Quotas for Jewish Refugees

When the Nazis came to power in Germany in 1933, they introduced anti-Semitic policies that ultimately culminated in the Holocaust. In an effort to escape these policies, many Jewish refugees fled Germany during the 1930s, but quota restrictions prevented thousands of them from coming to America. However, there was a movement in the United States aimed at lifting the quota restrictions to accommodate the victims of Nazi oppression. In 1939, Senator Robert Wagner cosponsored the Wagner/Nourse Rogers Bill, which would have temporarily allowed German refugee children to live with American families. Wagner hoped that by admitting only children, the bill could evade the objections of anti-immigrant opponents who feared that adult immigrants would flood America's labor market and increase unemployment rates. Ultimately, however, the Wagner/Nourse Rogers Bill did not become law. The text of the bill and Senator Wagner's remarks in support of it are reprinted below.

Whereas there is now in progress a worldwide effort to facilitate the emigration from Germany of men, women, and children of every race and creed suffering from conditions which compel them to seek refuge in other lands; and

Whereas the most pitiful and helpless sufferers are children of tender years; and

Whereas the admission into the United States of a limited number of these children can be accomplished without any danger of their becoming public charges, or dislocating American industry or displacing American labor; and

Whereas such action by the United States would constitute the most immediate and practical contribution by our liberty-loving people to the cause of human freedom, to which we are inseverably bound by our institutions, our history, and our profoundest sentiments: Now, therefore, be it

Resolved, etc., That not more than 10,000 immigration visas may be issued during each of the calendar years 1939 and 1940, in addition to those authorized by existing law and notwithstanding any provisions of law regarding priorities or preferences, for the admission into the United States of children 14 years of age or under, who reside, or at any time since January 1, 1933, have resided, in any territory now incorporated in Germany, and who are otherwise eligible: Provided, That satisfactory assurances are given that such children will be supported and properly cared for through the voluntary action of responsible citizens of responsible private organizations of the United States, and consequently will not become public charges.

Senator Wagner's Plea

The statements presented by Mr. Wagner are as follows:

The joint resolution I have just introduced authorizes the admission into the United States of 10,000 German refugee children of every race and creed, during each of the calendar years 1939 and 1940.

Millions of innocent and defenseless men, women, and children in Germany today, of every race and creed, are suffering from conditions which compel them to seek refuge in other lands. Our hearts go out especially to the children of tender years, who are the most pitiful and helpless sufferers. The admission of a limited number of these children into the United States would release them from the prospect of a life without hope and without recourse, and enable them to grow up in an environment where the human spirit may survive and prosper.

This resolution does not suspend existing quota restrictions on the immigration of adults. It merely authorizes the admission during a limited period of a limited number of refugee children, 14 years of age or under. This could readily be accomplished without their becoming public charges and without any danger of dislocating American industry or displacing American labor. Their admission would be predicated on satisfactory and voluntary undertakings by responsible American citizens or private organizations that adequate provision would be made for their maintenance and care in homes of their own faiths.

"A Token of Our Sympathy"

Thousands of American families have already expressed their willingness to take

German children flee Nazi persecution with all they can carry.

refuge children into their homes. Recently 49 of the outstanding Catholic and Protestant prelates of the United States, including His Eminence Cardinal Mundelein, joined in a statement urging our people to join together without regard to race, religion or creed in offering refuge to children as a token of our sympathy and as a symbol of our faith in the ideas of human brotherhood. Both branches of the labor movement have now joined in expressing sympathy for this objective.

Such action by the United States would follow the precedent of England and Holland, which have given sanctuary to many of these unfortunate victims of persecution. It would constitute our most immediate and practical contribution to the cause of human freedom, to which we are inseverably bound by our institutions, our history, and our profoundest sentiments. I have every confidence that there will be prompt and wholehearted response throughout the country to this noble cause, whereby the American people will give expression to their innermost cravings for liberty, justice, and international peace.

Wagner/Nourse Rogers Bill. February 9, 1939.

The Internment of Japanese Americans

The lives of Japanese Americans were irrevocably altered on December 7, 1941, when the Japanese government bombed the U.S. naval base at Pearl Harbor, Hawaii. Following the attack, anti-Japanese sentiment in the United States skyrocketed, and Americans feared that Japan might launch an invasion of the West Coast. Fears that Japanese Americans might collaborate with the Japanese government were used to justify the relocation of Japanese Americans in 1942 from their homes to internment camps in barren inland areas. In the following selection, Asian American activist Yuri Kochiyama recalls the day her family was sent to an internment camp in Arkansas and describes what life was like there.

Everything changed for me on the day Pearl Harbor was bombed. On that very day—December 7, the FBI came and they took my father. He had just come home from the hospital the day before. For several days we didn't know where they had taken him. Then we found out that he was taken to the federal prison at Terminal Island [in Southern California]. Overnight, things changed for us. They took all men who lived near the Pacific waters, and had anything to do with fishing. A month later, they took every fisherman from Terminal Island, sixteen and over, to places—not the regular concentration camps—but to detention centers in places like South Dakota, Montana, and New Mexico. They said that all Japanese who had given money to any kind of Japanese organization would have to be taken away. At that time, many people were giving to the Japanese Red Cross. The first group was thirteen hundred Isseis— my parent's generation. They took those who were leaders of the community, or Japanese school teachers, or were teaching martial arts, or who were Buddhist priests.

Japanese Americans line up for dinner at an internment camp. Many Japanese Americans were relocated to such camps after America entered World War II.

Those categories which would make them very 'Japanesey', were picked up. This really made a tremendous impact on our lives. My twin brother was going to the University at Berkeley. He came rushing back. All of our classmates were joining up, so he volunteered to go into the service. And it seemed strange that here they had my father in prison, and there the draft board okayed my brother. He went right into the army. My other brother, who was two years older, was trying to run my father's fish market. But business was al-ready going down, so he had to close it. He had finished college at the University of California a couple of years before. . . .

You could see the hysteria of war. There was a sense that war could actually come to American shores. Everybody was yelling to get the 'Japs' out of California. In Congress, people were speaking out. Organizations such as the Sons and Daughters of the Golden West were screaming 'Get the "Japs" out.' So were the real estate people, who wanted to get the land from the Japanese farmers. The war had whipped up such a hysteria that if there was anyone for the Japanese, you didn't hear about it. I'm sure they were afraid to speak out, because they would be considered not only just 'Jap' lovers, but unpatriotic. . . .

Most Japanese Americans had to give up their jobs, whatever they did, and were told they had to leave. The edict for 9066— President Roosevelt's edict for evacuation—was in February 1942. We were moved to a detention center that April. . . .

We were fortunate, in that our neighbors, who were white, were kind enough to look after our house, and they said they would find people to rent it, and look after it till we got back. But these neighbors were very, very unusual.

We were sent to an assembly center in Arcadia, California, in April. . . . Most of the assembly centers were either fairgrounds, or race tracks. So many of us lived in stables and they said you could take what you could carry. We were there until October.

Even though we stayed in a horse stable, everything was well organized. Every unit would hold four to six people. So in some cases, families had to split up, or join others. We slept on army cots, and for mattresses they gave us muslin bags, and told us to fill them with straw. And for chairs, everybody scrounged around for carton boxes, because they could serve as chairs. You could put two together and it could be a little table. So it was just makeshift. . . .

I was so red, white and blue [American], I couldn't believe this was happening to us.

America would never do a thing like this to us. This is the greatest country in the world. So I thought this is only going to be for a short while, maybe a few weeks or something, and they will let us go back. At the beginning no one realized how long this would go on. I didn't feel the anger that much because I thought maybe this was the way we could show our love for our country, and we should not make too much fuss or noise, we should abide by what they asked of us. . . .

At the beginning, we didn't have any idea how temporary or permanent the situation was. We thought we would be able to leave shortly. But after several months they told us this was just temporary quarters, and they were building more permanent quarters elsewhere in the United States. All this was so unbelievable. A year before we would never have thought anything like this could have happened to us—not in this country. As time went by, the sense of frustration grew. Many families were already divided. The fathers, the heads of the households, were taken to other camps. In the beginning, there was no way for the sons to get in touch with their families. Before our group left for the detention camp, we were saying goodbye almost every day to other groups who were going to places like Arizona and Utah. Here we finally had made so many new friends—people who we met, lived with, shared the time, and gotten to know. So it was even sad on that note and the goodbyes were difficult. Here we had gotten close to these people, and now we had to separate again. I don't think we even thought about where they were going to take us, or how long we would have to stay there. When we got on the trains to leave for the camps, we didn't know where we were going. . . . By October, our group headed out for Jerome, Arkansas, which is on the Tex-Arkana corner. . . . When we got to Jerome, Arkansas, we were shocked because we had never seen an area like it. There was forest all around us. And they told us to wait till the rains hit. This would not only turn into mud, but Arkansas swamp lands. That's where they put us—in swamp lands, surrounded by forests. It was nothing like California. . . .

There were army-type barracks, with two hundred to two hundred and five people to each block and every block had its own mess hall, facility for washing clothes, showering. It was all surrounded by barbed wire, and armed soldiers. I think they said only seven people were killed in total, though thirty were shot, because they went too close to the fence. Where we were, nobody thought of escaping because you'd be more scared of the swamps—the poisonous snakes, the bayous. Climatic conditions were very harsh. Although Arkansas is in the South, the winters were very, very cold. We had a pot bellied stove in every room and we burned wood. Everything was very organized. We got there in October, and were warned to prepare ourselves. So on our block, for instance, males eighteen and over could go out in the forest to chop down trees for wood for the winter. The men would bring back the trees, and the

women sawed the trees. Everybody worked. The children would pile up the wood for each unit. . . .

We always called the camps 'relocation centers' while we were there. Now we feel it is apropos [appropriate] to call them concentration camps. It is not the same as the concentration camps of Europe; those we feel were death camps. Concentration camps were a concentration of people placed in an area, and disempowered and disenfranchised. So it is apropos to call what I was in a concentration camp. After two years in the camp, I was released.

Joann Faung Jean Lee, ed., *Asian American Experiences in the United States: Oral Histories of First to Fourth Generation Americans from China, the Philipines, Japan, India, the Pacific Islands, Vietnam, and Cambodia.* Jefferson, NC: McFarland, 1991, pp. 10–18.

Chinese Americans as a "Model Minority"

The following selection is excerpted from a 1966 U.S. News & World Report *article in which the newsmagazine praises the low crime rates and strict family discipline found among Chinese Americans. The* U.S. News *article was one of many to describe Chinese Americans as a* model minority. *At a time when many Americans were participating in the civil rights movement, the article claims, the Chinese were working hard to overcome poverty and other hardships on their own.*

Visit "Chinatown U.S.A." and you find an important racial minority pulling itself up from hardship and discrimination to become a model of self-respect and achievement in today's America.

At a time when it is being proposed that hundreds of billions be spent to uplift Negroes and other minorities, the nation's 300,000 Chinese-Americans are moving ahead on their own—with no help from anyone else.

Low Rate of Crime

In crime-ridden cities, Chinese districts turn up as islands of peace and stability.

Of 4.7 million arrests reported to the Federal Bureau of Investigation in 1965, only 1,293 involved persons of Chinese ancestry. A Protestant pastor in New York City's Chinatown said:

"This is the safest place in the city."

Few Chinese-Americans are getting welfare handouts—or even want them. Within a tight network of family and clan loyalties, relatives continue to help each other. Mrs. Jean Ma, publisher of a Chinese-language newspaper in Los Angeles, explained:

"We're a big family. If someone has trouble, usually it can be solved within the family. There is no need to bother someone else. And nobody will respect any member of the family who does not work and who just plays around."

Today, Chinese-American parents are worrying somewhat about their young people. Yet, in every city, delinquency in Chinatown is minor compared with what goes on around it.

Strict Discipline

Even in the age of television and fast automobiles, Chinese-American children are expected to attend school faithfully, work hard at their studies—and stay out of trouble. Spanking is seldom used, but supervision and verbal discipline are strict.

A study of San Francisco's Chinatown noted that "if school performance is poor and the parents are told, there is an immediate improvement." And, in New York City, schoolteachers reportedly are competing for posts in schools with large numbers of Chinese-American children.

Recently Dr. Richard T. Sollenberger, professor of psychology at Mount Holyoke College, made a study of New York City's Chinatown and concluded:

"There's a strong incentive for young people to behave. As one informant said, 'When you walk around the streets of Chinatown, you have a hundred cousins watching you.'"

What you find . . . is a story of adversity and prejudice that would shock those now complaining about the hardships endured by today's Negroes.

It was during California's gold rush that large numbers of Chinese began coming to America.

On the developing frontier, they worked in mines, on railroads and in other hard labor. Moving into cities, where the best occupations were closed to them, large numbers became laundrymen and cooks because of the shortage of women in the West.

Past Handicaps

High value was placed on Chinese willingness to work long hours for low pay. Yet Congress, in 1882, passed an Exclusion Act denying naturalization to Chinese immigrants and forbidding further influx of laborers. A similar act in 1924, aimed primarily at the Japanese, prohibited laborers from bringing in wives.

In California, the first legislature slapped foreign miners with a tax aimed at getting Chinese out of the gold-mining business. That State's highest court ruled Chinese could not testify against whites in court.

Chinese-Americans could not own land in California, and no corporation or public agency could employ them.

These curbs, in general, applied also to Japanese-Americans, another Oriental minority that has survived discrimination to win a solid place in the nation.

The curbs, themselves, have been discarded in the last quarter century. And, in recent years, immigration quotas have been enlarged, with 8,800 Chinese allowed to enter the country this year.

As a result, the number of persons of Chinese ancestry living in the United States is believed to have almost doubled since 1950.

Today, as in the past, most Chinese are to be found in Hawaii, California and New York. Because of ancient emphasis on family and village, most of those on the U.S. mainland trace their ancestry to communities southwest of Canton.

How Chinese Get Ahead
Not all Chinese-Americans are rich. Many, especially recent arrivals from Hong Kong, are poor and cannot speak English. But the large majority are moving ahead by applying the traditional virtues of hard work, thrift and morality.

Success stories have been recorded in business, science, architecture, politics and other professions. Dr. Sollenberger said of New York's Chinatown:

"The Chinese people here will work at anything. I know of some who were scholars in China and are now working as waiters in restaurants. That's a stopgap for them, of course, but the point is that they're willing to do something—they don't sit around moaning."

The biggest and most publicized of all Chinatowns is in San Francisco. . . .

"Streets Are Safer"
A University of California team making a three-year study of Chinatown in San Francisco reported its impression "that Chinatown streets are safer than most other parts of the city" despite the fact that it is one of the most densely populated neighborhoods in the United States.

In 1965, not one San Francisco Chinese—young or old—was charged with murder, manslaughter, rape or an offense against wife or children. Chinese accounted for only two adult cases out of 252 of assault with a deadly weapon.

Only one of San Francisco's Chinese youths, who comprise 17 per cent of the city's high-school enrollment, was among 118 juveniles arrested last year for assault with a deadly weapon. Meantime, 25 per cent of the city's semifinalists in the California State scholarship competition were Chinese. . . .

Much the same picture is found in mainland America's other big Chinatowns—Los Angeles and New York. . . .

A police lieutenant said:

"You don't find any Chinese locked up for robbery, rape or vagrancy."

There has been some rise in Chinese-American delinquency in recent years. In part, this is attributed to the fact that the ratio of children in Chinatown's total population is going up as more women arrive and more families are started.

Even so, the proportion of Chinese-American youngsters getting into difficulty remains low. School buildings used by large numbers of Chinese are described as the cleanest in New York. Public recreational facilities amount to only one small park, but few complaints are heard. . . .

Over all, what observers are finding in America's Chinatowns are a thrifty, law-abiding and industrious people—ambitious to make progress on their own.

U.S. News & World Report, December 26, 1966.

Growing Up Arab in America

In the account below, Arab American Mojahid Daoud articulates the difficulty many immigrants experience in trying to figure out their personal identity. Daoud's father came to America in 1952, and although Daoud was born in the United States, for much of his youth he struggled to decide whether he was an Arab or an American. Eventually, Daoud writes, he decided it was possible to be both.

Daoud's struggle is similar to what many immigrants and their children expe-rience, but as an Arab American, Daoud was especially affected by world affairs, primarily the conflicts in the Middle East. Daoud sympathized with Arab efforts to take Palestinian lands back from Israel, whereas most Americans support Israel. This division, writes Daoud, made him feel even more like an outsider.

When I started elementary school my parents realized that the name Mojahid Daoud simply would not be appropriate for my early school years. The other kids would in all likelihood not learn how to pronounce the name and, even if they did (four or five pronunciations later), they would probably laugh at it. Or so we thought. Consequently, I was given Mark David as a school name—which was to remain my name throughout adolescence. It was not an insignificant change. I would not stand out as different from the other kids. This eventually served to lessen my identity as an Arab. . . .

My parents were always cognizant [aware] of the importance of not alienating their children from the American kids. If it meant relinquishing our identities as Arabs, they were willing to sacrifice that for our happiness. This was not easy for them. It was not as though their escape from the overwhelming poverty of Jordan led them to want to relinquish all remnants of their life there. They were very proud Arabs who had strong familial and religious ties to their country of birth. Despite their improved lot in the United States, America was to be only a vehicle by which they could return to Jordan and resume their lives there. . . .

However, despite my parents' strong ethnic pride and their attempts to make us proud Arabs, my brother and I rejected our heritage. We felt that we did not want to be different from Americans and that, if we asserted our identity, we would never be accepted. Furthermore, we felt that our Arab culture was backward compared to American culture. Our return to Jordan in 1972, supposedly to live there for good, only solidified these beliefs. We returned to a country so poor and destitute, having been wracked by a civil war, that we knew we would never make our home there. We went from playing kickball and swimming in our neighbor's pool to playing in open sewers and seeing lambs sacrificed before our eyes. It was too much for a child my age to cope with. We came back to the United States to resume our disrupted lives. . . .

By the time I began high school, I was fully adjusted to American life. I had many friends and was fairly well known to all my classmates. I played football and was able to make the all-league first team as guard. At the same time, I felt more and more distant from my Arab past. I had no Arab friends and the ones that I did know did not understand my experiences. I just wanted to fit in with my classmates.

Nevertheless, I still knew my place in the school as an Arab. I was constantly referred to as sand-nigger and camel jockey, even by teachers that I knew. At the time, I just shrugged off the remarks because I thought that they were directed at me and not my culture. I just felt that the guys were joking around. I knew little of the political undertones that had produced this mindset. . . .

I entered the University of Cincinnati in the fall of 1979. Things did not change much as far as my orientation to my ethnicity was concerned. I lived, ate, and drank with Americans, and they remained my only frame of reference for judging the world. I was having a great time American-style, and I was not about to change it. But that orientation was drastically altered with the Israeli invasion of Lebanon in 1982. Up until that time my political awareness was lacking, and I still faithfully believed in American politics. That, however, quickly dissolved after viewing, night after night, Israel's massive bombardment of Lebanon, with America's blessing. My human spirit was being tested as I realized that I could not sit idly by. I decided that I had to make myself aware of what was occurring. I suddenly realized that those were my brothers and sisters who were being terrorized day after day.

I started to get involved with the other Arabs at the university who were activists in the Palestinian [Arab] cause. They became very close and proved to be good friends who would do just about anything for me. At the same time, I began to distance myself from my American friends who were still the way I once was, mainly interested in having a good time. . . . Obviously, people go through changes but this one I felt would be too much for my friends to handle. This was probably a mistake because ultimately I never gave my friends the chance to accept this new dramatic dimension in my life. . . .

In the summer following my graduation, I went back to Jordan to, as they say, rediscover myself. The first time I visited had been a terrible experience. We felt our parents were trying to take away something that we loved, namely our American identity. We could not understand what compelled my parents to want to return to Jordan. This time was different. Where the smell of goats and chickens had once offended me, it now became a cultural expression of our folklore. Where the simplicity of a farmer tilling the land with his oxen had appeared backward, it now seemed a romantic alternative to the mechanized, undefinable lifestyle of the United States. What I had really come to terms with was the fact that, in some way, I was witnessing myself and my past. I was not ashamed of it as I once was. I was proud to be from this naked land. . . .

Following my return from Palestine and Jordan, my consciousness was reshaped. I had developed a pride in my Arab past so great that I considered myself not an American, as I once did, but an Arab. Much was a result of my social relationships with other Arabs. However, my raised political consciousness was the most important reason why I began to change . . . in the service of my fellow man. I enrolled in the urban planning program at the University of Michigan. . . .

I have finally stopped deluding [fooling] myself as to who I am. Early in my life, it was so important for me to be accepted in this society as an American that I rejected my ancient heritage. Later on, as I became more politically conscious and aware of the beauty of traditional Arab life, it became important for me to be recognized as an Arab, to the point of even rejecting my American identity. In each instance, the feeling of alienation impelled [forced] me to choose one side, instead of integrating [combining] the two. I still ask myself why it is necessary to be forced to choose.

Baha Abu-Laban and Michael W. Suleiman, *Arab Americans: Continuity & Change.* Belmont, MA: Association of Arab-American University Graduates, 1989.

Torn Between Two Cultures

Mai Lin is a Taiwanese American whose parents moved the family to America in 1978, when she was ten years old. In the following interview, conducted in 1989 when she was a student at the Massachusetts Institute of Technology, Lin describes her struggle to maintain an American lifestyle while also honoring her Chinese heritage. She says that as a child she only wanted to be American, but as a young adult she has rediscovered Chinese culture. She wonders what will happen if she has children, and whether she will be able to teach them the Chinese language and customs that she values.

Interviewer: You're now a citizen [of the United States]. How do you see yourself, as half of your life was in Taiwan, really, and half of it's been here?

Lin: Up until my freshman year in college I had denied the fact that I was Chinese. I just wanted to be American, and it was all I cared about. I didn't care to know about Chinese history. I didn't care [about] my relatives. I didn't really want to know. I didn't even want to know what was happening in my own country. But since I've been at M.I.T., I've been a lot more aware. I have started to take Chinese history courses and literature. I want to go back and learn Chinese again. So I'm struggling with the fact that I am Chinese and that I am American in my lifestyle and everything else I do, but a lot of internal values I have are still Chinese.

So why is this a struggle?

Anything that is in me that's Chinese is also tied to my parents, and I'm still having a hard time with my parents, even though we get along better now. I still feel very guilty at times for what they've gone through and what they're still going through.

When I try to define what's Chinese versus what's American and trying to get what's good out of each, it's very difficult. Socially there's different things that are a little difficult. For myself it's certainly a lot more difficult to be an adolescent trying to survive two different cultures. Here the women are just different from Chinese women. Chinese women are supposed to be a lot more quiet and subdued and submissive. Not that you go out of your way

to do that, but they just come across that way. In my family it's always been the females who have been the stronger ones. But then just the fact that I also have to take that image and fit myself into this image that Americans have about their women: that they're thin, they're blond—blond is beautiful—blue-eyed, and fair-skinned, although they try to tan themselves. It's been difficult. As an adolescent trying to choose what was right from which culture—it wasn't just growing up and trying to choose what's right and wrong. Here you're choosing what's right in which culture and what's wrong in which culture. It was always a struggle. It was certainly a lot more difficult than if I had either been an American or else just stayed in Taiwan.

If I do have kids here—well, depending on who my spouse is—if I end up marrying someone who is non-Chinese, how do I keep the culture going? Do I want to keep the culture going in the children? I think the one thing that's very important is the language. It's always good to be bilingual or trilingual, whatever you can to learn a different language. And so that if I want to keep the Chinese going, what do you do with your spouse unless they learn the language as well? It's not easy to instill that in your children, who are going to probably speak English most of the time.

And then just different things like the Chinese value of looking after your parents. Usually the son, the oldest son, is supposed to take care of the parents, but, you know, suppose my brother marries somebody who is non-Chinese? My mother isn't going to feel comfortable living with an American daughter-in-law. She's going to think that she's not going to know how to take care of them, and so then it will be up to me to kind of look after them. But suppose I marry someone who's non-Chinese?

I don't know. They're all questions I'm still trying to figure out.

June Namias, ed., *First Generation: In the Words of Twentieth-Century Immigrants*. Boston: Beacon Press, 1992.

Overcoming Racism

Since the Vietnam War, thousands of Hmong, a tribal people of Laos, have settled in California. Vu Pao Tcha is a Hmong American living in Fresno, a city with one of the largest concentrations of Hmong Americans in the United States. In this 1993 essay, written while he was attending the University of California at Santa Barbara, Tcha relates how surprised he was by the everyday racism he witnessed, which he says was often directed at immigrants but also occurred between immigrant groups. He also writes of his struggle to retain his Hmong heritage while embracing his life as an American. He suggests that his true identity is to be found in both cultures.

Fresno is a city with people of diverse ethnic backgrounds, of whom the majority is Euro-American, though there are a lot of blacks, Chicanos, and Central Americans,

too. There is also a large concentration of Asians, mostly Southeast Asians, a new group that has increased rapidly in recent years. Because of this large increase of minority groups in Fresno, especially of Southeast Asian refugees, a lot of tension arose between the old residents and the newcomers. Prejudice can often be observed, whether at school, in hospitals and shopping centers, or on the street.

One day, while I was driving home from school, a group of white boys riding in a pickup truck tried to intimidate me. They yelled and cursed at me. They gave me the finger and screamed a four-letter word repeatedly. I heard them say, "Go back home! This is our country!"

Then they spat at me and laughed. One of them even pointed his finger at me as if he were shooting at me. I could hear him laugh and say, "Bang! Bang! You're dead, you f—Hmong."

I had witnessed similar violent actions toward other Asians before, so I knew they were just trying to intimidate me. Instead of reacting angrily, I took a turn and disappeared. Of course I was shocked and angry, and I wanted to get back at them, but I held my temper. I knew that if I tried to get revenge, I would be just as inhumane as they were. My father has always taught me to be tolerant. He said that revenge only makes things worse. I agree.

Many of my friends who could not tolerate the racism against our community in Fresno have become racists themselves. They have often provoked other groups, usually whites, into bloody fights. As a result, their actions not only heightened the reaction against us but have also brought a negative image to our community. Revenge is definitely not the answer to racism.

Indeed, racism was the first shocking thing I observed after my arrival in the United States. It was very common to witness racist actions against minority groups by Euro-Americans. However, it was also not unusual at all to observe the same kind of tension among different minority groups themselves. In Fresno, it was very rare to see minorities around whites, but it was even rarer to see minority groups interacting with each other.

Racism was probably the hardest challenge and most difficult obstacle that I've encountered in the United States. . . .

I believe I am living an American life with an American dream today. Yet it's still hard for me to consider myself an "American." Why? Is it because there is a part of me that is not American at all? Is it because I look different? Yes and no. I have no definite answer. But what is an American? What does it mean to be an American—especially an Asian American? I agree with what my Asian American peers tell me: although I am Asian and look Asian, I am not an Asian of Asia any more. I am no longer a Hmong of the mountains of Laos. I no longer hold strong Hmong cultural values. What I once treasured is no longer important to me. Now, could I ever live the mountain life again if I go back to Laos? It's very unlikely. Since I'm no longer totally

Hmong, nor am I a real American, what am I?

I believe that being an American means being something different from what I used to be, having different values, and living a different life. People who choose to make the United States their home are Americans because they have chosen to live differently from their ancestors. They have become something different—something new. Of course, they can never be completely like other Americans because there are so many different Americans. There are different kinds of Euro-Americans just as there are different kinds of Asian Americans and Afro-Americans. In short, Americans can never be completely alike even if

Two young members of the Hmong community who will face the challenges of assimilation.

they are all Americans because America is a country of diverse people.

It is harder to deny my new identity than to accept it. I know I have become an American even though I am different from other Americans. Whether I like it or not, I am a new Asian American—a Hmong American. So why not make that my identity?

Hello, my fellow Americans!

Sucheng Chan, ed., *Hmong Means Free: Life in Laos and America*. Philadelphia: Temple University Press, 1994.

CHAPTER FOUR

The Immigrant Experience Since the 1960s

The second great wave of immigration to the United States ended during the early 1920s. During that decade, anti-immigrant sentiments led Congress to pass a series of laws that limited the number of immigrants allowed into the United States each year. These laws also instituted a quota system, known as the National Origins System, that limited the number of immigrants that would be allowed each year from specific countries. This quota system greatly favored immigrants from northern and western Europe.

The quota system, along with the Great Depression and World War II, worked to dramatically reduce the flow of immigrants into the United States. For example, although more than 1 million immigrants came to the United States between 1929 and 1945, more than 10 million had arrived between 1900 and 1910.

Following the passage of the Immigration Act of 1965, which ended the National Origins System, a new wave of immigration began. Since 1970, more than three-quarters of legal immigrants have come from developing nations in Latin America, the Caribbean, and Asia. The United States is experiencing a third great wave of immigration. The documents in this chapter provide insight into the modern immigrant experience.

A Nation of Immigrants

President John F. Kennedy, himself the grandson of immigrants, opposed the quota system (known as the National Origins System) that governed U.S. immigration policy from the 1920s to the early 1960s. He viewed the quota system's preference for white immigrants as racist. In his 1963 book A Nation of Immigrants, *Kennedy called for a reform of immigration laws. He advocated making immi-*

President John F. Kennedy wanted to make an immigrant's ability to contribute to the American economy the determining factor for issuing an immigration visa.

grants' ability to contribute to the American economy, rather than their country of origin, the primary factor in deciding whether they should be granted an immigration visa. In the aftermath of Kennedy's assassination in 1963, Congress passed the Immigration Act of 1965, *which broadened admission to peoples from all continents.*

The Immigration and Nationality Act of 1952 undertook to codify all our national laws on immigration. This was a proper and long overdue task. But it was not just a housekeeping chore. In the course of the deliberation over the Act, many basic decisions about our immigration policy were made. The total racial bar against the naturalization of Japanese, Koreans and other East Asians was removed, and a minimum annual quota of one hundred was provided for each of these countries. Provision was also made to make it easier to reunite husbands and wives. Most important of all was the decision to do nothing about the national origins system.

The famous words of [poet] Emma Lazarus on the pedestal of the Statue of Liberty read: "Give me your tired, your poor, your huddled masses yearning to breathe free." Until 1921 this was an accurate picture of our society. Under present law it would be appropriate to add: "as long as they come from Northern Europe, are not too tired or too poor or slightly ill, never stole a loaf of bread, never joined any questionable organization, and can document their activities for the past two years."

Furthermore, the national origins quota system has strong overtones of an indefensible racial preference. It is strongly weighted toward so-called Anglo-Saxons, a phrase which one writer calls "a term of art" encompassing almost anyone from Northern and Western Europe. . . .

Yet, however much our present policy may be deplored, it still remains our national policy. As President Truman said when he vetoed the Immigration and Nationality Act (only to have that veto overridden): "The idea behind this discriminatory policy was, to put it boldly, that Americans with English or Irish names were better people and better citizens than Americans with Italian or Greek or Polish names. . . . Such a concept is utterly unworthy of our traditions and our ideals." . . .

There is, of course, a legitimate argument for some limitation upon immigration. We no longer need settlers for virgin lands, and our economy is expanding more slowly than in the nineteenth and early twentieth centuries. A superficial analysis of the heated arguments over immigration policy which have taken place since 1952 might give the impression that there was an irreconcilable conflict, as if one side wanted to go back to the policy of our founding fathers, of unrestricted immigration, and the other side wanted to stop all further immigration. In fact, there are only a few basic differences between the most liberal bill offered in recent years . . . and the supporters of the status quo. . . .

The clash of opinion arises not over the number of immigrants to be admitted, but over the test for admission—the national origins quota system. Instead of using the discriminatory test of where the immigrant was born, the reform proposals would base admission on the immigrant's possession of skills our country needs and on the humanitarian ground of reuniting families. Such legislation does not seek to make over the face of America. Immigrants would still be given tests for health, intelligence, morality and security. . . .

Religious and civic organizations, ethnic associations and newspaper editorials, citizens from every walk of life and groups of every description have expressed their support for a more rational and less prejudiced immigration law. Congressional leaders of both parties have urged the adoption of new legislation that would eliminate the most objectionable features of . . . the nationalities quota system. . . .

The Presidential message to Congress of July 23, 1963, recommended that the national origins system be replaced by a formula governing immigration to the United States which takes into account: (1) the skills of the immigrant and their relationships to our needs; (2) the family relationship between immigrants and persons already here, so that the reuniting of families is encouraged; and (3) the priority of registration [those who register earliest for immigration should receive priority]. . . .

These changes will not solve all the problems of immigration. But they will insure that progress will continue to be made toward our ideal and toward the realization of humanitarian objectives.

We must avoid what the Irish poet John Boyle O'Reilly once called

Organized charity, scrimped and iced, in the name of a cautious, statistical Christ.

Immigration policy should be generous; it should be fair; it should be flexible. With such a policy we can turn to the world, and to our own part, with clean hands and a clear conscience. Such a policy would be but a reaffirmation of old principles. It would be an expression of our agreement with George Washington that "The bosom of [America is] open to receive not only the opulent and respectable stranger, but the oppressed and persecuted of all nations and religions; whom we shall welcome to a participation of all our rights and privileges, if by decency and propriety of conduct they appear to merit the enjoyment."

John F. Kennedy, *A Nation of Immigrants*. New York: Anti-Defamation League of B'nai B'rith, 1963.

Seeking a Higher Education

Today, many immigrants come to America in search of educational opportunities unavailable in their native countries. Such was the case for Tunde Ayobami, a Nigerian who came to the United States in 1969, when he was twenty-one. In the following account, Ayobami describes his decision to move to America and his arrival in Rhode Island. Unlike many Nigerians coming to the United States for school and then returning home, Ayobami chose to stay.

I knew about the U.S. while I was growing up, because I did have a lot of friends. I mean Americans who came to Nigeria to teach, mostly white.

We met and we exchanged addresses, magazines, things like this. This was while I was in the high school. They tell me all the things about America, all good things. So I was keen to come in here.

My father, of course, he didn't want me to go anywhere. Because for one thing, I'm the number one in the family and I'm supposed to take care of everybody. He was thinking of when he dies; who is going to be the head of the family. But, by the same token, he always respect my individual decision. Well, I said I'm going to travel out to the U.S.

I have a friend—then he was about fifteen years old—I'm talking about white American family, from Bristol, Rhode Island. We got in touch through the ham radio operation. Then we started to write each other. And when I was coming here and I didn't have any money, he sent some money to me. It was 1969, and I was about twenty-one. I come with the idea of just going to school and going back; because, for one thing, I didn't know what to expect. I just knew what I was going to do: Go to school, get my degree, and go back. . . .

I landed in JFK and I found my way to Rhode Island, to the family. Oh, they are wonderful. That's my American mother and father. She was a marvelous woman. That's why I call her mom, even up to now. I stayed with them for two months. Within this two months, I was introduced to all kind of people. Everybody want to see our picture together, everything like that. There was a big write-up in the *Bristol Journal*. And I met the reverend of the church, and everything.

The family has a small construction business and I helped them out. And I was working as a gardener in Mrs. Marjory Carruthers's. She was really rich. I was mowing the lawn with the lawnmower taking care of the flowers.

I was disappointed for the fact that the money wasn't easy to get. Judging from the Hollywood pictures and how people were smashing cars and everybody walk leisurely on the street, I thought I was going to a paradise; you don't have to earn money. [*Laughs.*]

After a couple of months I found a school, Bristol Community College. . . .

I got involved in different things, and I got to meet different people. I was a Sunday School teacher. It was the Baptist church in Fall River, and I'd go there every Sunday. A wealthy lady, she bought a bike for me, and I went to church on my bike. I was teaching the tenth and twelfth graders. I had a lot of talks, you know—interviews and talk shows—I'd go to the Kiwanis, the deacon's lunch. I talked about Africa and business in Africa and how Americans can come to Africa, and all these kind of things.

I was the first Nigerian in the area. Before I came here, none of us [Nigerians] had the idea of going to the suburbs. New York, Boston, Philadelphia—big cities. When I go to visit them, they say, "Where

are you, anyway? I never heard of the place. We'll come to see you sometime." So they come and stay over the weekend; and we travel around, I show them places. Most of them didn't know any other place but New York City. But I tell them this place is really peaceful. And when they come to Rhode Island, I try to find jobs for them and find school at the same time. They pay less money for the school, which is an attraction. And I introduced a lot of Nigerians to the church. So everybody come, and most of them have been able to finish school and go to wherever they want to go.

When I finished Bristol Community College, I applied to four-year colleges. I got an admission to Southeastern Massachusetts University, and that was where I went. I finished my college program—medical technology. After I finished school, I got interviews from different companies, and this company hired me. I was in the lab, doing hematology. It was a good job. You know, the lab is always interesting. But the moment you are not given an opportunity to do anything—you know, like management changes and everybody has different ideas—and when the company say, "Well, this is the way we're going to stay," it became so boring staying in the lab, because we do the same thing every time. So I decided to leave the lab and get into sales, technical sales. . . .

I went to the boss and I said, "I don't want to be in the lab. I want to get into sales somewhere." He said there was no position, but later I found out it was because he didn't think I would ever make a good salesman. Most people didn't think I would make it. First, because of my accent; then said I would never sell anybody.

So I was waiting for the best time to quit the company. But the management changed, and the new guy, the vice-president, thought it was a good idea to challenge everybody who wants to do something, so I got into the sales field. I'm one of the first black employees in sales in my company. In my division, I'm the first one. In another department there is another one—not African.

Now I'm a technical sales rep, and what I do—besides make money for the company—is to go to some customers. My territory includes Pennsylvania, Illinois, Minnesota, Wisconsin, Indiana. Maybe an average of two days a week I'm not home. But it depends on planning. I like it. I like it very much. The territory was dying before I took it over, and now the sales has been going up, up, up, up, up. Since I've been on the road, my territory has been improved about 200 percent. The vice-president just wrote me a note, congratulating me. He said, "Keep it up."

Joan Morrison and Charlotte Fox Zabulsky, eds., *American Mosaic*. New York: E.P. Dutton, 1980.

Finding Fame in the United States

Rennie Stennett grew up in Panama before coming to the United States in 1969 to play professional baseball. From 1971 to 1981 he enjoyed fame as a major league pitcher. In this account Stennett re-calls experiencing racism when he came to America and being struck by Americans' obsession with money.

The [baseball] scouts been coming since I was in eighth grade, trying to get me to finish school in the United States. They always come down, looking for guys, good ballplayers. The club I was going to sign with at first was the [San Francisco] Giants, because they used to come every year. The guy would come to my home and talk to my mother and father, take me all over Panama, and stuff like that. They wanted to bring me over here and I think they was going to pay my schooling, plus I play baseball for that team. Of course, I wanted to play, but my dad, he tell me he want me to at least finish high school.

I guess it was about the last four months in school when I started thinking professional. The [Pittsburgh] Pirates came just before I got out of high school, and that was perfect time. And they offered me a little bit more than the other club. So I went with them.

It was really tough at first. First of all, where I grew up there was black and white lived there, and we go to same church and everything and no problems. We never had the kind of race problem they had here [in America]. I knew about it by the newspapers. So when I came here, I didn't even speak to a white person. . . . Sometimes I used to get hate mail. You know, people call me names and stuff like that.

My first year I didn't play league [major league baseball]. I played in the minor leagues, Class A. I hate riding buses, but I know it was worth it. Well, in the minors you don't have the beautiful ball parks to play in; the lights are not strong, and they're throwing the ball hard—they don't know where it's going. You have those coaches trying to teach you, but you've got to make it on your own. It was tough. You is the one got to make that adjustment and groom yourself. And when they think you're ready, they'll bring you up to the big leagues.

Well, I'd played in the minor league that year, and just after the season—see, the minor league only play four months—I went back there [Panama]. I want to continue my education, to get credits meanwhile, and I went into a junior college. I was going into physical ed, something that I can be good in. And then I had a chance to work, so I decided to do that, too.

They were interviewing different people for a job on the [Panama] Canal. I was going—you know, regular shirt and pants. My father said, "Well, you're going for a job, you shouldn't go like that. You should have on a tie." I didn't have much, but I put it on and it really worked, because most of the other guys got the jobs lifting up things, and since I was in a tie, they asked me if I ever did any kind of accounting or anything like that. I didn't, but I tell them I could do it. And that's why I got that job, as a checker on the dock. That's the person that check the items that come off the dock, like different foods and radios and different things. I had a list with what's supposed to be on the ships, and I was to check those. . . .

The second year I played with Class A again. The third year I jumped to Triple A. At the half of the season I came to the big leagues. Some guys take about seven and eight years to get to the big leagues, but I was lucky. I did it in two and a half. . . .

Of course, I read so many things about America. All I had the impression is just money. Whenever it come around to money, the American will be the smartest person in the world, and he will do anything, even kill. That's the impression I get by the movies. Every movie, it's the same—if it's a Western or whatever it is, you will see when it come round to getting that money, the American will be the smartest and toughest, even if it kills him to get the money. This is what it projected in Panama. And then it seems like when I come over, I think it's the same way. You know, you got to have money. Over here a lot of people say, "Hey, you're nothing unless you got money."

Nowadays most people like to meet me because of who I am. I make a lot of money. So I have to be a little on my guard all the time, to find out if the person likes me for me or just for what I am or what I have. That's very important to me.

Joan Morrison and Charlotte Fox Zabulsky, eds., *American Mosaic*. New York: E.P. Dutton, 1980.

Staying in America or Returning Home: A Difficult Choice

More than twenty-four thousand Indians immigrated to the United States between 1966 and 1970, one-third of them classified as "professional, technical, or kindred workers." In 1977 one of these skilled workers, an anonymous scientific researcher, gave the interview excerpted below. In it, he explains that he initially planned to come to America to get a college degree and then return home. But after graduation, he decided to work for a few years to gain some experience in his field. The researcher weighs the benefits of remaining in America against the obligations he has to his family and his country to return home to India. Many immigrants, especially those with family abroad, face this choice.

After a year of working [in India] I wanted to go for higher studies and I really wanted to go to an advanced country just to look around and see how the things are. I got this admission and assistantship [in the United States], but at that point my father died, in '63, early '64—I had some family responsibilities.

The structure in India is somewhat different than what you have here. I had my sisters who were not married, and marriage is a big deal there. I decided that I could not leave the responsibility I had for the family. So I completely cooled the idea of going for several years.

Then in '68 it occurred to me that maybe I should go out, maybe write to this university and see what they say now. I wrote back to them. They provided assistance. I said, "I'll go and study there two or three years and see how things go." . . .

Naturally I talked it over with the family. . . . My mother was somewhat skepti-cal about it; she did not think I should go, but knowing that I had waited for so many years, and she is very negotiable, she really didn't object that much. My wife's parents were quite strong on this. They did not want us to go away and forget India completely. They had a feeling that we would not come back—come back in the sense of living there permanently. But we talked it over with them and basically they understood that I am going to fulfill my ambition—I'll not stay for long. And there was no main difficulty in convincing my wife; we had good communication. The child was only three years old, so we didn't have to ask him.

In the beginning, somehow it didn't look like to me a great step. . . .

Interviewer: How come you stayed here after you got your degree?

My feeling was that going to school was good—it gave me a certificate, gave me some background, all right. But I didn't get any idea about how the industry's operating. I planned to be in the area of research for the rest of my life. I really thought for me to take advantage of my stay here I really ought to work, really to get the first-hand experience. And then we decided I would work about three, four years and then go back.

I thought that three years is a long period originally. But you know, three years really gets you started and that's the reason we really have to postpone it. If [the visa is good until 1980] it gives me six, seven, eight years of working [here]. . . .

Vietnamese citizens rush to board an American embassy bus to escape from South Vietnam.

I am saying we are planning to go back in '80, '81. I am not saying that we have got a plane ticket and we will go. We will probably review at that time. But I think if we decide not to go at that time then we are here for good. . . .

Would you say from the point of view of India, the Indian economy, they have lost a great deal?

I feel that the point that the country has been losing a lot has been overemphasized. First of all, the way I think, I don't think the country has lost a heck of a lot if I stay away eight years and come back with better training. In fact they may come out winner.

June Namias, ed., *First Generation: In the Words of Twentieth-Century Immigrants*. Boston: Beacon Press, 1992.

A Vietnamese Success Story

Lang Ngan is one of approximately eighty-thousand Vietnamese who were evacuated from South Vietnam after that country surrendered to North Vietnam in 1975. Ngan was evacuated because she had worked for the U.S. embassy in South Vietnam. When the evacuation began, she was given little notice and had to round up her immediate family quickly and secretly leave for the airport. In the selection below, Ngan describes how she and her family arrived in New York with very little money. However, through hard work, sacrifice, and good fortune, they eventually prospered.

My sister and I left . . . first, and we started work as soon as we got to New York. We started looking for apartments, but at the time, my salary was only one hundred fifty dollars a week, and my sister made one hundred twenty-five dollars. Someone took us to look for an apartment in Flushing, Queens. A two bedroom was two hundred fifty dollars, and a one bedroom was one hundred ninety dollars, and even with a family of nine, we took the one bedroom, because we tried to save as much as possible. Fortunately, the building superintendent was a refugee—from Cuba—and he helped us. He said he wouldn't tell the landlord that there were nine people living there as long as we didn't make any noise, and kept the children quiet. So he helped us get the apartment. He lied to the landlord for us by saying there were only two girls in the apartment—my sister and myself. The superintendent was very helpful. He tried to get some used furniture for us, and used clothes and dishes. He collected them from other tenants and his friends. That is how we started.

Half a month later, we had the rest of our family join us. Even though there was only my sister and I working to support nine, life wasn't bad. We were quite happy. But the only frustration was our parents. They had a lot of difficulty adjusting. They felt isolated, because there were no Can-tonese-speaking people in the building, and in the daytime, when all the children were in school, there was nothing for them to do but sit. In the beginning, I wanted to go back to Vietnam, because life was easier there. Here, we had no friends or relatives, and the lifestyle was so different. Even the mailbox was different. Every evening, we opened it and it was full of papers and envelopes. I was afraid to throw away anything in case it was important, so I would read every word—thinking they were letters—not realizing that this was advertising, junk. . . .

The first books we bought were dictionaries. We got three or four of them. We used them a lot. We didn't have any friends or relatives here, but at least we were together as a family. The children studied very hard to catch up in school. We had only one table, and they all had to study together around the same place, and all of them still feel this closeness to this day. We helped each other. I helped the children at that time, but not now. Now they correct my accent.

We had no furniture—just a few chairs and a used sofa that the supervisor gave us, and broken TV. And the rest were mattresses. We had no beds, only mattresses. In the evening, we had to carry all the mattresses to the living room for the males to sleep. All the females slept in the bedroom. And we lived in this condition for two and a half years, until we were able to get a two-bedroom apartment. We waited till we felt financially secure to do this. We had saved money over the two and a half years, and because I was getting married, I felt that with my husband's income, we could afford to move. My husband and I got a one bedroom apartment and my family moved to a two bedroom place in the same building. We were very happy. We felt that we were one family unit. We were really together, and sharing. There was no privacy, but we all remembered the times we had gone through together, and we were able to work things out with each other without problems.

All my younger sisters and brothers have done very well in school. And the teachers and school counselors have shown them what is the best way for them to go. Actually, we didn't give them that much counseling. They got it all from school. Even though they don't act the same way I did when I was going to school in Vietnam, they still have certain values—such as respect, and obeying teachers, and therefore the teachers liked them, and tried to help them. My sister got a full scholarship to MIT from Bell Labs. I have one brother who got an electrical engineering degree from Columbia, and the other finished at City College. One other brother is going to medical school at New York Med.

I think the problems we had when we first came to this country helped our success. We're not like other people who were born here, and had everything. We went through all those difficulties, so when we have a chance, we grab it. We now own a two family house. My husband and I live in one side, my parents in the other.

Joann Faung Jean Lee, ed., *Asian American Experiences in the United States: Oral Histories of First to Fourth Generation Americans from China, the Philippines, Japan, India, the Pacific Islands, Vietnam, and Cambodia*. Jefferson, NC: McFarland, 1991.

Greedy About Life Again

For Wong Chun Yau, a woman who emigrated from Communist China in 1979 when she was sixty years old, coming to the United States was a profoundly uplifting experience. In the selection below she describes the political oppression that was common during the 1940s, '50s, and '60s under Communist leader Mao Tsetung. Yau had been wealthy in China, and therefore became a target in Communist crackdowns against the privileged elite of society.

I look back at my life in China and I get scared. Now my life is worth something; it is precious again. In the past, I felt so what if I am shot, I just die. There wasn't anything to live for, anyway. But now, I am greedy about life again. I want to live.

My daughter lived in San Francisco, so that's where I went when I arrived in this country in 1979. I was sixty years old.

In China, I owned two houses. And if you had money in China, it was a crime. If you were an intellectual, it was a crime. The really poor, who didn't have a thing, they were the average, so no harm came to them. But if you had a cent, they would purge [try to get rid of] you. If you owned land, they would purge you. I was purged by the Red Guards twice. This was in the 1960s. Every time they had some movement, they would drag me out, and make me the center of the event. They took everything—my money, my furniture. Even now the furniture hasn't been returned. They beat me—took off my jacket and beat me. I was sick for three months after that. They stuck me in a cow pen. And then they kept telling me to list my crimes. In the mornings, when I got up, I would have to write. But what could I say? I didn't kill anyone, or set any fires. So what was I supposed to write? So they told me to write down all the things I did against humanity. But I couldn't figure out what I did against the people. I was never a thief or anything. It was a very painful period. . . .

My husband swam to Hong Kong in 1962, and then all my children swam out of China into Hong Kong in 1967. Then they came to this country as refugees in 1970. But I didn't leave China until 1979 when my son petitioned to have me join him in America.

When I was in my forties I followed some local guys trying to make the break. I am a good swimmer so I swam for almost three hours to the outer territories of Hong Kong, and I saw this fishing boat, so I asked to get on board, thinking, I am so close, this must be a Hong Kong ship. But as it turned out, the fisherman was from China, and he took me back because he could get [money] for returning me to the government. So I was purged and beaten, and beaten and purged. They even took a

knife and stabbed me in my face. I still have this scar where they split open my mouth.

Things are fine now in this country [America]. I want to live to be one hundred. In China, I always wanted to die. There was hardly anything to eat and you had to work all day. If you wanted one particular thing, you couldn't get that particular thing. You could get only one dollar's worth of meat a month. And a dime's worth of fish a month. And even with the dime, you couldn't always find fish to buy. . . . Everything required ration tickets. Rice, bread, congee, everything required tickets. What's great about this country is I can buy a whole loaf of bread and even pastries and not need a ration ticket for them. Just the idea of being able to order a bowl of noodles, and not have to give a rice ticket—it's fabulous.

Joann Faung Jean Lee, ed., *Asian American Experiences in the United States: Oral Histories of First to Fourth Generation Americans from China, the Philippines, Japan, India, the Pacific Islands, Vietnam, and Cambodia*. Jefferson, NC: McFarland, 1991.

A Single Mother Faces Poverty and Deportation

Between 1977 and 1981, roughly sixty thousand Haitian immigrants came to the United States, fleeing the poverty and political turmoil in Haiti. Many of them settled in a Miami, Florida, community now known as Little Haiti. The following account is by Paulette Francius, a Haitian who immigrated to the United States illegally in 1983. Francius settled in Little

Haiti and had three children with a man who later left her. In this (translated) account, Francius worries about what will happen to her. She does not speak English and has been unable to find a job while also taking care of her children. She says that her life is marked by poverty and the threat of violence, but that it is nevertheless better than her previous life in Haiti.

When Americans talk to me, I can understand some words, but I cannot comprehend exactly what they are saying. If I had someone to watch the kids, I would take English class. At home, I can't even learn English from watching television, because the kids are usually running around. I know how to count in English, and the days of the week. That's about all.

In the four years I've been in Miami, I've had limited contact with Americans. I only see Haitian people. I am afraid of Americans. Robbers come into people's houses with guns and say "Give us everything you have, or we will kill you." It's happened many times on this street. A thief came into my next-door neighbor's apartment just this week, but the lady was home and heard the noise. She ran outside, yelling for help.

Many times, thieves come when everyone is asleep and steal even decorations on window ledges. That is why we all have iron bars on our windows. And I make sure to lock my door every night. The robbers are both Haitians and black Americans. The Liberty City neighborhood is seven blocks away. That's a pretty rough area. What can we do? The white police can beat us up, and the blacks come in and rob us. . . .

I don't know what will happen to me. My immigration case is still on appeal before the judge. Periodically I am called into the INS [Immigration and Naturalization Service] building for the judge to ask if what I have already told them is true. But they still haven't scheduled my final hearing. If my plea fails, they can send me back to Haiti. My children are American citizens, because they were born in Miami. They would leave with American passports and could come back any time. But I wouldn't be able to come with them. My hope is for the children to go to school, so they can become *someone.*

I am very worried about my status, but I don't like to complain while I am in this country, because the American government has given me food to eat. They provide medical care and enough money to pay the rent. In Haiti, there is no welfare program or American-style clinic for the children.

I worry. Not about these children's future: I believe that nothing bad will happen to them. But I worry about my son in Haiti. He is eleven years old now. I would like to send money to my mother to take care of him or to send for him, but I cannot afford to. And my mother is very poor. She sent me a letter recently and asked me to take him. The government took some of her land and left her without anything. In Haiti, there is no justice.

I have no regrets about coming to Miami. Even though my life is uncertain, I have food. I can say anything I want to say.

There are no Macoutes or police who bother me. Still, I miss my relatives and wish that I could do more for them.

If I could find work now, I would be happy. Any type—on a farm, in town—it doesn't matter. But I can't look for work, because in this neighborhood there is only one day-care center, on 22nd Avenue. You have to sign a waiting list. It takes two years, sometimes they forget about you. And a requirement for day care is that you must already be working. They won't take children if the parent is trying to find a job. Where does that leave me?

Al Santoli, *New Americans: An Oral History.* New York: Viking Penguin, 1988.

The United States Makes Restitution for the Internment of Japanese Americans

In 1988 the U.S. government formally recognized the injustice of the internment of Japanese Amerians during World War II. That year Congress passed legislation that provided restitution payments to the surviving Japanese Americans who had been interned and to their descendants. President Ronald Reagan's remarks on the signing of the legislation are excerpted below.

The Members of Congress and distinguished guests, my fellow Americans, we gather here today to right a grave wrong. More than 40 years ago, shortly after the bombing of Pearl Harbor, 120,000 persons of Japanese ancestry living in the United States were forcibly removed from their homes and placed in makeshift internment camps. This action was taken without trial, without jury. It was based solely on race, for these 120,000 were Americans of Japanese descent.

Yes, the Nation was then at war, struggling for its survival and it's not for us today to pass judgment upon those who may have made mistakes while engaged in that great struggle. Yet we must recognize that the internment of Japanese-Americans was just that: a mistake. For throughout the war, Japanese-Americans in the tens of thousands remained utterly loyal to the United States. Indeed, scores of Japanese-Americans volunteered for our Armed Forces, many stepping forward in the internment camps themselves. The 442d Regimental Combat Team, made up entirely of Japanese-Americans, served with immense distinction to defend this nation, their nation. Yet back at home, the soldiers' families were being denied the very freedom for which so many of the soldiers themselves were laying down their lives.

Congressman Norman Mineta, with us today, was 10 years old when his family was interned. In the Congressman's words: "My own family was sent first to Santa Anita Racetrack. We showered in the horse paddocks. Some families lived in converted stables, others in hastily thrown together barracks. We were then moved to Heart Mountain, Wyoming, where our entire family lived in one small room of a rude tar paper barrack." Like so many tens of thousands of others, the members of the

Mineta family lived in those conditions not for a matter of weeks or months but for 3 long years.

The legislation that I am about to sign provides for a restitution payment to each of the 60,000 surviving Japanese-Americans of the 120,000 who were relocated or detained. Yet no payment can make up for those lost years. So, what is most important in this bill has less to do with property than with honor. For here we admit a wrong; here we reaffirm our commitment as a nation to equal justice under the law.

Ronald Reagan, Remarks on Signing the Bill Providing Restitution for the Wartime Internment of Japanese-American Civilians, August 10, 1988.

Hispanic Americans' Experience with Assimilation

Linda Chavez is a Hispanic American who has served as staff director of the U.S. Commission on Civil Rights. She currently serves as president of the Center for Equal Opportunity, a conservative think tank. In 1992 Chavez gave a speech in which she discussed the experience of Hispanic American immigrants. In the excerpts of that speech reprinted below, Chavez expresses her belief that it is important for Hispanic Americans to assimilate into mainstream American society. She argues that bilingual education, in which Hispanic American students are taught in their native language until they learn English, could hinder the assimilation process, which would make it harder for Hispanic Americans to achieve economic and social success.

The face of America is changing—becoming more diverse and complex than at any time in our history. We're no longer a white-and-black society struggling to integrate two major groups of people who have been in this country for nearly four hundred years, but a multiracial, multiethnic society in which newcomers are arriving in record numbers every day. The 1980s will be remembered as a period of one of the highest levels of immigration in our nation's history. Some ten million persons immigrated to the United States in the last decade, a number as great as that of the peak decade, 1900 to 1910.

Unlike the immigrants of the early part of this century who were primarily from Europe, the great bulk of the last decade's immigrants—approximately eighty percent—were from Asia and Latin America. Much has been made of this phenomenon and many who favor restricting immigration suggest that these new Asian and Latin immigrants will be less successfully absorbed into the fabric of American society. . . .

Hispanic Americans Are Prospering

But, in fact, when we look at one of these groups, we find that most Hispanics are assimilating the social, educational, economic, and language norms of this society despite the image of Hispanics portrayed in the media and perpetuated by Hispanic leaders. Let me just acquaint you with a few facts about the Hispanic population with which you may not be familiar:

• Mexican-origin men have the highest labor-force participation rates of any group, including non-Hispanic whites and Asians.

• U.S.-born Hispanics have rapidly moved into the middle class. The earnings of Mexican-American men are now roughly eighty percent of those of non-Hispanic white men.

• Mexican-Americans with thirteen to fifteen years of education earn, on an average, ninety-seven percent of the average earnings of non-Hispanic white males.

• Most differences in earnings between Hispanics and non-Hispanics can be explained by educational differences between the two groups, but at the secondary-school level, young Mexican-Americans are closing the gap with their non-Hispanic peers. Seventy-eight percent of second-generation Mexican-American men aged twenty-five to thirty-four have completed twelve years of school or more, compared with approximately ninety percent of comparable non-Hispanic whites.

• English proficiency is also key to earnings among Hispanics, but here, too, conventional wisdom about Hispanics is mostly invalid. The overwhelming majority of U.S.-born Hispanics are English-dominant, and one half of all third generation Mexican-Americans—like most other American ethnics—speak only one language: English.

• What's more, Hispanics, with the exception of Puerto Ricans, have marriage rates comparable to those of non-Hispanic whites. Three quarters of Mexican-origin, Cuban, and Central and South American Hispanics live in married-couple households. And nearly half own their own homes.

If these facts come as a surprise to you, it's largely because most of the analyses of Hispanics fail to note that nearly half of the adult Hispanic population is foreign-born. And like new immigrants of the past, Hispanic immigrants will take at least one generation to move up the economic ladder and into the cultural mainstream.

The Struggle to Assimilate

Perhaps a little history lesson is in order. The current period is not the only time in our history during which we have viewed new immigrants with distrust and suspicion. We tend to forget that Italians, Greeks, Jews, Poles, and others—whom some people lump together as "Europeans"—were considered alien to the white Americans of the early twentieth century, most of whom were of British, German, or Scandinavian descent. . . . For anyone who believes that immigrants of an earlier day lived in a halcyon [pleasant] time of tolerance and acceptance among their fellow white European-descended Americans, I recommend a few hours of reading through the reports of the 1921 Dillingham Commission, which in 1924 ultimately recommended a quota system to keep out southern and eastern European immigrants and Asians.

The point is that immigrants have never had it particularly easy in this society, nor have they always been welcomed with open arms, despite [poet] Emma Lazarus's words on the base of the Statue of Liberty. ["Give me your tired, your poor, / Your huddled masses yearning to breathe free."] Nonetheless, most of those who came here from other countries found the struggle worth the effort. And these groups did, by and large, succeed in America.

Today, Italians, Jews, Poles, Greeks, and others of southern and eastern European background are virtually indistinguishable from so-called native-stock Americans on measure of earnings, status, and education. Even Chinese and Japanese Americans, who were subject to much greater discrimination than southern and eastern Europeans, have done exceedingly well and outperform most other groups on all indicators of social and economic success. But it took three generations for most of these groups to achieve this status. . . .

Is it possible, then, simply to mimic what we did in the past in treating this generation of newcomers? No. Let me concede that we did a great deal of wrong in the past, and immigrants succeeded in spite of, not because of, our mistakes. It would be neither compassionate nor legal to return to a system in which we put non-English-speaking children into public-school classrooms in which the instruction was entirely in English and expect those children to "sink or swim." In 1974 this approach was declared by the United States Supreme Court to violate our civil rights laws. Nor should we harken back to the "good old days" when Anglo conformity was the sole acceptable cultural model.

The Importance of a Common American Culture

But in trying to right past wrongs, we should be careful not to reverse ourselves 180 degrees by attempting to educate each group of immigrant children in their own native language and inculcate [mold] them in their own native culture. . . . If we insist on separate language instruction for all immigrant students—167 different languages are spoken in New York alone—we will close the door on integration, divide ourselves along cultural/linguistic lines, and thereby perpetuate inequalities rather than eradicate them. . . .

Those Hispanics who wish to maintain their native language and culture—and polls show that a majority of Hispanic immigrants do—should follow the example of their fellow ethnic Americans by establishing their own cultural societies by which to do so. Frankly, given the tremendous diversity within the Hispanic community, the only successful way for each group to ensure that its members know its history and traditions is to undertake that education itself. If government is entrusted with the responsibility, it is likely to amalgamate [combine] and homogenize [mix different elements into a uniform culture] in ways that make the original culture virtually indecipherable.

The government, after all, is capable of lumping all twenty-two million Hispanics in this nation into one category—a category that includes Cakchikel Indians from Guatemala, mestizos [people of mixed European and American Indian ancestry] from Mexico, the descendants of Italian immigrants from Argentina, Japanese immigrants from Peru, Spaniards from Europe, and the descendants of colonists who settled the Southwest nearly four hundred years ago. Wouldn't it be better to entrust each of these very different groups with the responsibility of maintaining its own traditions without the interference—or assistance—of the government?

Some critics warn that the United States is in danger of fragmenting into competing racial and ethnic groups. Historian Arthur Schlesinger, Jr., has called it the "disuniting of America." No doubt, our task is more complicated today than at any time in the recent past. Nonetheless, I remain optimistic that we can—if we commit ourselves—successfully integrate the more than seventy million blacks, Hispanics, Asians, and American Indians into our society. That we can create a new *unum* [one] out of the many already here and the many more who are to come.

But to do so will require the cooperation of us all—those who have been here for generations as well as those who are coming each day. It will require that each of us recognizes the covenant [agreement] that exists between the old and the new: that we respect the rights of individuals to maintain what is unique in their ancestral heritages, but that we understand that our future is in forging a common identity of shared values and beliefs essential to the democratic ideal.

Linda Chavez, *Historic Preservation Forum*, January/February 1993.

Rafting to Freedom

Ernesto Reina was born in Havana, Cuba, in 1970. He made four attempts to leave the island but was captured each time. Then in 1994, Cuban premier Fidel Castro said that anyone who wanted to leave Cuba could do so. Reina and his friends were among tens of thousands of Cubans who built homemade rafts and set sail for the United States. Reina kept a journal of his experiences, portions of which are excerpted below. In them Reina speaks of America in glowing terms as a land of freedom and opportunity.

I couldn't believe my ears, I just couldn't believe it. Fidel Castro had announced that he would let anyone who tried to leave the island go free. Everyone in Cuba was talking about the same thing. At first, I thought that it was another one of his evil lies, but no, people I knew had taken the trip to freedom and no one had stopped them. This was my opportunity; the fifth time would be the charm.

I had tried four times to go to the U.S. but besides being unsuccessful I was arrested on three occasions. I spent time in Fidel's jail cells: eighteen months, six months and 3 months, respectively. On the fourth try, I avoided imprisonment thanks to a bribe of 3,000 pesos. Now the fifth adventure was about to begin. . . .

Sunday, August 14

11:30 a.m. I got together with a few friends at a house belonging to one of our fellow rafters. No one was older than 25. Nervous, but hopeful, we decided that the time had come to flee to the U.S. We planned everything quickly. We bought, on the black market, naturally, six innertubes from truck tires to help keep us afloat. Six innertubes would be enough. Manuel, one of our "companeros", [companions] promised to bring the rafts and the rope which we would use to construct the deck of our "vessel". I would contribute the board, Fidel [another companion] would provide a sheet—that could be used as a sail. Each one got whatever necessary items he could find for the difficult crossing. . . .

Tuesday, August 16

6:00 p.m. The fight to attain freedom has a very high price and I was about to pay it. At my house, my wife and my five month old son were sleeping. With a broken heart, I gave a little kiss to "Ernestico"—that's what I like to call him—I didn't want to wake my wife so as not to upset her. Perhaps, many people wouldn't understand why I left them behind but I did it for them and for myself. If my dream of arriving safe and sound in Miami came true, I could struggle and work in order to have them join me, and in this way, become the happiest man in the world.

7:30 p.m. I met the rest of my friends on the beach. We are all prepared for the adventure that could cost us our lives, but could also allow us to be born again. With ropes, cloth and innertubes, we managed to construct a raft. The only "motor" it had would be the oars and our own strength. One out of four. This was not a bet. These

odds keep churning in my mind. For every four rafts launched into the sea, only one reaches its goal. The other three become food for the sharks or are swallowed up by the sea, overturned in a storm. At the moment of departure, I remember that my wife, who has a good memory for dates, told me that today would be the second anniversary of Hurricane Andrew, the storm that left Florida looking as limp as my sock. . . .

Wednesday, August 17

1:00 p.m. Fourteen miles off Cuban shore, the raft turned over. It was a terrible experience. We lost the few provisions that we had and everyone fell into the water. We ended up without anything to drink. If necessary we were ready to refresh our throats with salt water. We thought that would be the end, but fortunately, after much painful effort, we managed to get onto the raft again.

At this terrible moment I recalled once again the hair-raising stories that were circulating among the people of Havana about the many who had made the crossing and lost their lives on the high seas, about the empty rafts found by the American Coast Guard, about the sharks who ate the rafters. This last fear is one that I can speak of from experience. A shark began to circle around the innertube where I was sitting. A shark's fin appears harmless. It is green, the color of hope, and black, like death. Everyone knows that sharks prefer to attack white objects. Sharks are nearsighted and can only see objects that are white and bright. . . .

Using a homemade raft, Cuban refugees flee Communist dictator Fidel Castro.

In our hurry to leave we hadn't been able to rub the raft down with gasoline, which would have warded off those dangerous fish. Fear was running through my veins at the same time that I was bursting with energy—from who knows where—to keep on struggling. In the end we didn't have any problem with that darn shark who miraculously disappeared from alongside our raft.

3:30 p.m. The only part of our bodies that we could move without fear of falling back into the sea was our heads. Anxious and impatient, we would look in all directions hoping to spy a boat that would rescue us from that endless wait. . . .

Suddenly I spotted a black point on the horizon that looked like a ship. Shouting, I alerted my companions. When we saw the black dot, we were exhilarated. Tears came to my eyes. Without worrying that it might be an optical illusion, I threw my first flare and then the second. A precarious and nervous happiness came over us.

4:00 p.m. Half an hour later, I had used the third and last flare. Thank God, as it approached, the black dot turned out to be a United States Coast Guard launch. We looked at each other with tears in our eyes, and our lips broke into smiles of joy, that until then had been lost. . . .

4:30 p.m. Finally, we were rescued. The eighteen hours of danger and agony had been rewarded with the marvelous prize. Our transfer from the raft to the enormous Coast Guard vessel was symbolic of the huge change that we were making in our lives. It was stepping from the past into the present. A present that, for us, was full of promise. Our future needed only to begin. . . .

Friday, August 19

However, as I said before, my goal does not end with reaching freedom in the U.S.A. Now I am working hard in order to save enough money to send for my family. I want them to know what life is like in "paradise."

Ernesto Reina, *Seven Days: Diary of a "Rafter."* 1994.

INDEX

DISCOVERING MATH

FRACTIONS

DAVID L. STIENECKER

ART BY RICHARD MACCABE

BENCHMARK BOOKS

MARSHALL CAVENDISH

NEW YORK

Benchmark Books
Marshall Cavendish Corporation
99 White Plains Road
Tarrytown, New York 10591-9001

©Marshall Cavendish Corporation, 1996

Series created by Blackbirch Graphics, Inc.

Library of Congress Cataloging-in-Publication Data

Stienecker, David.
    Fractions / by David L. Stienecker.
        p. cm. — (Discovering math)
    Includes index.
    Summary: Includes an assortment of activities and illustrations to help explain the concept of fractions.
        ISBN 0-7614-0598-4 (lib. bdg.)
        1. Fractions—Juvenile literature. {1. Fractions.} I. Title.
    II. Series.
    QA117.S75   1995   95-12425
    513.2'6—dc20   CIP
                                                     AC

Contents

■ ■ ■ ■ ■ ■ ■

Alphabet Flags

Many ships carry a set of flags that stand for the letters of the alphabet. This system of alphabet flags is called the international flag code. Here is what the alphabet flags look like.

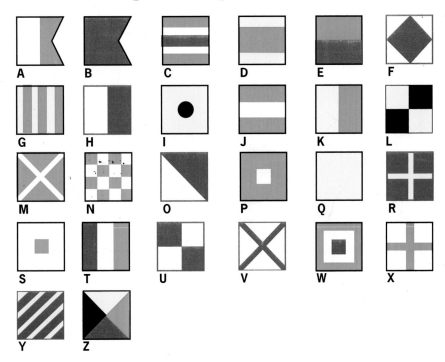

Sailors can use the flags to spell out words. Usually, they use certain flags for warnings or messages.

Take this O-flag, for example. It is divided into two equal parts. One half is yellow and one half is red. When this flag is raised it means someone has fallen overboard!

If a ship flies this L-flag, it means, "You should stop. I have an important message." How many equal parts is this flag divided into? Write a fraction to show how much of the flag is black, and how much is yellow.

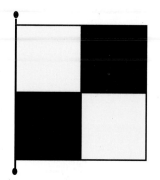

A fraction is a part of a whole.

If a ship is having trouble steering, it flies this D-flag. Write a fraction to show what part of the D-flag is blue. Write a fraction to show what part is yellow.

This C-flag by itself stands for "yes." How many equal parts is it divided into? Write fractions to show how much of the flag is blue, how much is red, and how much is white.

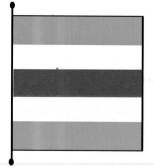

- Look at some of the other alphabet flags. Write fractions to show how the flags are colored. Drawing the flags may help you decide.

- Use the alphabet flags to spell out your name.

Dividing Shapes

Try this activity with a friend. First trace each of the shapes. Then follow the directions for dividing each shape into equal parts.

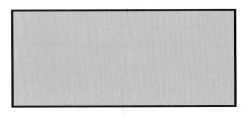

Find three ways of dividing this rectangle into four quarters.

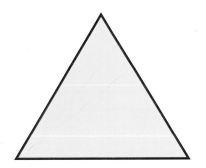

Divide this triangle into four equal parts. Then try dividing it into six equal parts. Folding your paper or using a ruler might help you figure it out.

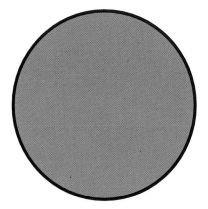

Divide this circle into four quarters. Then divide it into eighths. Folding may be the easiest way.

Find two different ways to divide this hexagon into three equal parts.

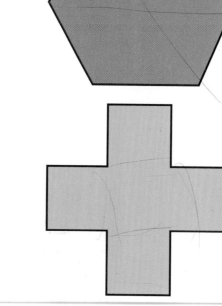

First divide this shape in half. Then into quarters. Then trace it again. Divide it into five equal parts. Then divide it into eighths.

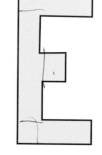

How can you cut this letter E into five equal parts? You may want to use a ruler to figure it out.

- See if you can find some more ways to divide the shapes above into equal parts.

- Make some shapes of your own. Then work with a friend to figure out how many ways you can divide the shapes into equal parts.

Tangram Puzzle

Almost 4,000 years ago the Chinese made a puzzle by cutting a square into seven pieces. The puzzle is called a tangram. These are the seven tangram puzzle pieces. Can you name the three different shapes?

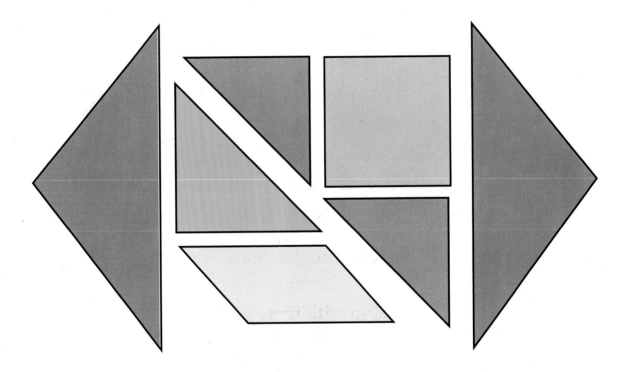

Many books have been written on the pictures and shapes you can make with the tangram pieces. You can even fit some pieces inside other pieces.

Carefully trace or copy the tangram pieces above onto a sheet of paper. Then cut them out and see if you can fit them inside the square on the next page. It may take a little time, but it works

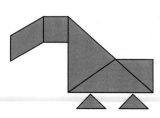

- Write a fraction on each piece to show what part of the square it is. It might help to lay one piece on top of another to determine its fractional part.

- Now have some more fun with these amazing tangrams. Make some pictures. You must use all seven pieces in each one.
  To get you started, here are a duck and a candlestick.

Fraction Card Games

Play the greatest fraction card game with a partner. You will need a deck of cards with the face cards removed. The aces stand for ones.

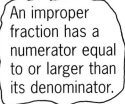

An improper fraction has a numerator equal to or larger than its denominator.

How to play:

- Shuffle the deck with the face cards removed.

- Deal each player four cards.

- Players use their cards to make a fraction. The player with the greatest fraction takes all the cards. If there is a tie, each player keeps his or her cards. No improper fractions please!

- Continue playing until all the cards have been used. The player with the most cards at the end of the game wins.

Here's how one hand of the game might work. These are the cards each player has been dealt.

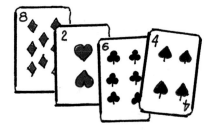

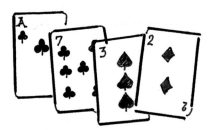

Player A

Player B

This is the largest fraction Player A can make with the four cards.

This is the largest fraction Player B can make with the four cards.

Player A's fraction is 6/8 which is the same as 3/4. Player B's fraction is 2/3. Three-fourths is larger than two-thirds, so Player A takes all eight cards.

If there is a dispute about which fraction is larger, use a calculator to change the fractions to decimals. Then compare the numbers.

Here are some variations on the game you might like to try.

- Play the smallest fraction game. Play the same way, but instead of making the greatest fraction, see which player can make the smallest fraction.

- Play the improper fraction game. Instead of making the greatest or smallest fraction, see who can make the largest improper fraction.

Invisible Picture

You say you don't see anything? Of course you don't. The picture is invisible until you draw lines to connect equivalent fractions. Use the dots as a guide.

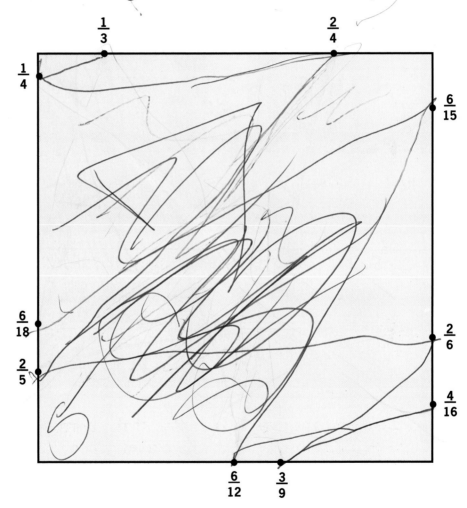

Did you find the star? Now that you understand how it works, use equivalent fractions to make some "invisible" pictures of your own.

Equivalent Fractions Game

Try this game, which is similar to the game of concentration. You'll need to make a deck of fraction cards like these:

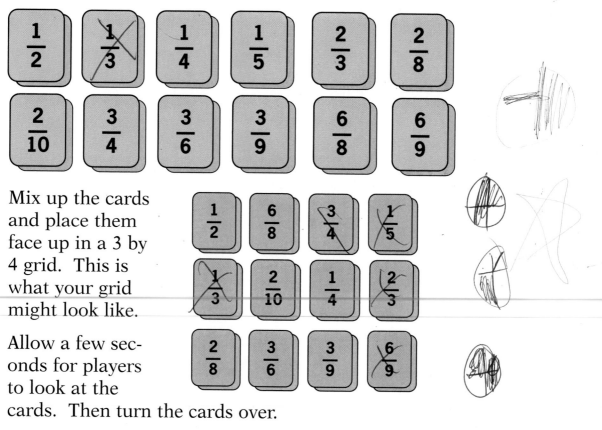

Mix up the cards and place them face up in a 3 by 4 grid. This is what your grid might look like.

Allow a few seconds for players to look at the cards. Then turn the cards over.

The first player flips over two cards. If the cards match as equivalent fractions, the player takes the cards and plays again. If not, the cards are turned over and the next player takes a turn.

The game continues until all the cards are removed. The player with the most cards wins.

- Try playing with more cards. Make two or three additional pairs of equivalent fractions.

13

All Sides Equal

What's the secret of this number triangle?

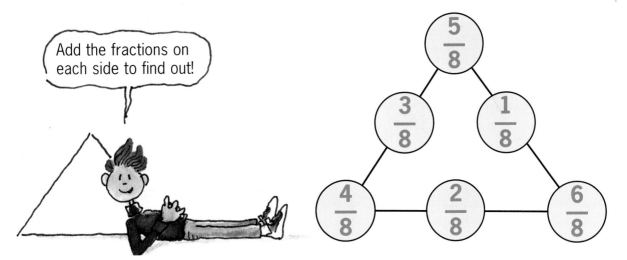

Add the fractions on each side to find out!

- Now draw a triangle like the one above. Find three more ways to arrange the fractions so each side equals 1½. Remember, use each fraction only once.

- Draw some more triangles. See if you can arrange the numbers ⅓, ⅔, 1, 1⅓, 1⅔, and 2 so each side equals 3. There is more than one solution. Work with a friend. See who can find a solution first.

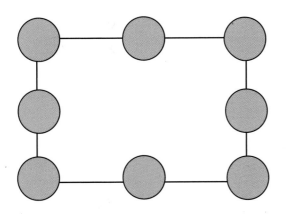

Here's a real challenge. Arrange the numbers ¼, 2/4, 3/4, 1, 1¼, 1 2/4, 1 3/4, and 2 in this rectangle so each side equals 3. Then arrange the numbers so that each side equals 3 ¾.

Fraction Magic Square

See if you can discover the magic in this magic square. First trace or make a copy of it.

A. **1**	B.	C.
D.	E.	F.
G.	H.	I.

The oldest-known magic square is over 4,000 years old.

Now solve each of the following problems. Reduce each answer to its simplest form. Then write the answers in the matching squares in the magic square. The first one is done for you.

A. $\dfrac{3}{5} + \dfrac{2}{5} = \dfrac{5}{5} = 1$

B. $\dfrac{7}{8} + \dfrac{6}{8} + \dfrac{5}{8}$

C. $\dfrac{7}{8} - \dfrac{3}{8}$

D. $\dfrac{11}{12} - \dfrac{2}{12}$

E. $\dfrac{3}{8} + \dfrac{7}{8}$

F. $\dfrac{6}{8} + \dfrac{5}{8} + \dfrac{3}{8}$

G. $\dfrac{3}{6} + \dfrac{4}{6} + \dfrac{5}{6}$

H. $\dfrac{9}{16} - \dfrac{5}{16}$

I. $\dfrac{1}{4} + \dfrac{2}{4} + \dfrac{3}{4}$

Now add up each row, column, and diagonal in the magic square. The magic is in the sums. What is it?

Fraction Blocks

If you know something about multiplying and dividing fractions, these building block puzzles will be a snap. Here's the key you'll need.

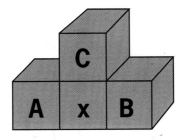

$$A \times B = C$$

This is how you use the key. Product block C sits on top of the two factor blocks, A and B. Always look for this arrangement of blocks.

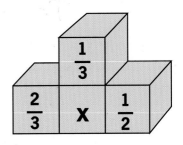

Are you ready? Remember, when you multiply fractions, just multiply the numerators and then the denominators, or the other way around.

- See if you can figure out the mystery number in these puzzles. Reduce your fractions when you can.

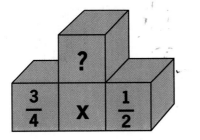

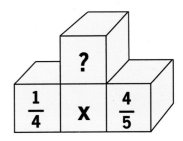

- These two puzzles are a little more difficult. You may want to use division to find the missing factors. It's up to you. Just remember, when you divide fractions, turn the divisor upside down and multiply.

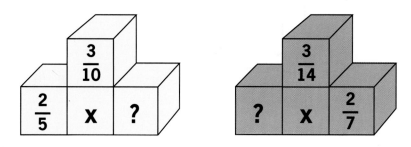

- Here are a couple of real whoppers. See if you can figure out all the mystery numbers. Sometimes you may want to multiply. Other times you may want to divide.

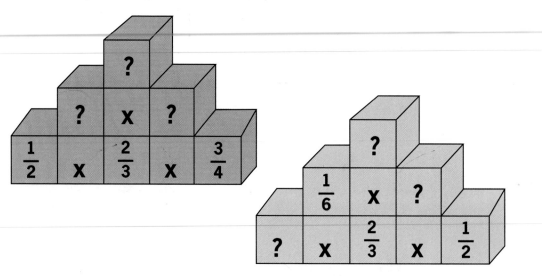

- Making up fraction block puzzles is as much of a challenge as the puzzles themselves. Try making a few of your own and giving them to friends to solve.

Fraction Code

Break the code. Solve the fraction problems in the decoder. Use the answers to solve the riddles below.

DECODER		
$\frac{1}{4} + , \frac{2}{4} =$ **A**	$\frac{2}{7} + \frac{3}{7} =$ **G**	$\frac{4}{15} + \frac{7}{15} =$ **N**
$\frac{1}{3} + \frac{1}{3} =$ **B**	$\frac{4}{11} + \frac{5}{11} =$ **H**	$\frac{4}{5} - \frac{3}{5} =$ **O**
$\frac{7}{8} - \frac{4}{8} =$ **C**	$\frac{5}{9} - \frac{3}{9} =$ **L**	$\frac{12}{13} - \frac{7}{13} =$ **R**
$\frac{15}{20} - \frac{6}{20} =$ **D**	$\frac{6}{10} - \frac{3}{10} =$ **M**	$\frac{6}{18} + \frac{9}{18} =$ **T**
$\frac{5}{12} - \frac{2}{12} =$ **E**		$\frac{6}{16} + \frac{3}{16} =$ **U**

How long should a cat's legs be?

$\frac{2}{9}$ $\frac{1}{5}$ $\frac{11}{15}$ $\frac{5}{7}$ $\frac{3}{12}$ $\frac{11}{15}$ $\frac{1}{5}$ $\frac{9}{16}$ $\frac{5}{7}$ $\frac{9}{11}$ $\frac{15}{18}$ $\frac{1}{5}$

$\frac{15}{18}$ $\frac{1}{5}$ $\frac{9}{16}$ $\frac{3}{8}$ $\frac{9}{11}$ $\frac{15}{18}$ $\frac{9}{11}$ $\frac{3}{12}$ $\frac{5}{7}$ $\frac{5}{13}$ $\frac{1}{5}$ $\frac{9}{16}$ $\frac{11}{15}$ $\frac{9}{20}$

What goes up a chimney closed, but can't go down a chimney open?

$\frac{3}{4}$ $\frac{11}{15}$ $\frac{9}{16}$ $\frac{3}{10}$ $\frac{2}{3}$ $\frac{5}{13}$ $\frac{3}{12}$ $\frac{2}{9}$ $\frac{2}{9}$ $\frac{3}{4}$

• Think up a fraction code of your own. Use it to send messages and solve riddles.

Sum and Product Game

Make two sets of number cards like these.

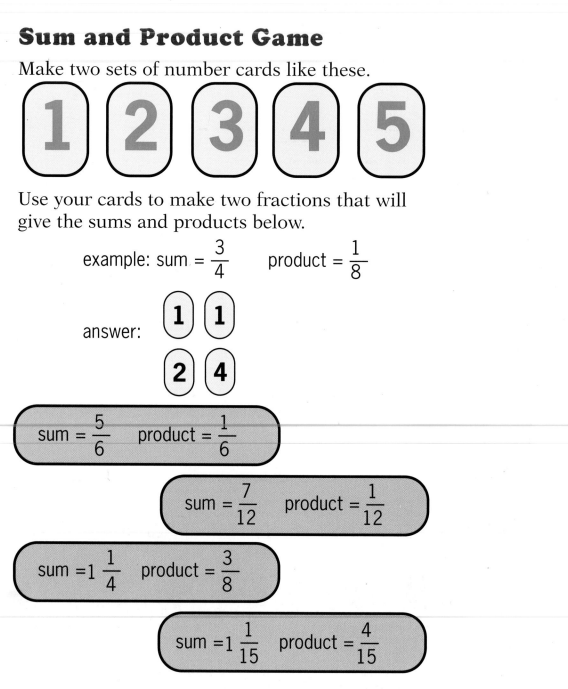

Use your cards to make two fractions that will give the sums and products below.

example: sum = $\dfrac{3}{4}$ product = $\dfrac{1}{8}$

answer: **1** **1**
         2 **4**

sum = $\dfrac{5}{6}$ product = $\dfrac{1}{6}$

sum = $\dfrac{7}{12}$ product = $\dfrac{1}{12}$

sum = $1\dfrac{1}{4}$ product = $\dfrac{3}{8}$

sum = $1\dfrac{1}{15}$ product = $\dfrac{4}{15}$

- See if you can make up some sum/product problems of your own. Use these cards or make a different set of cards.

19

Fraction Graph Pictures

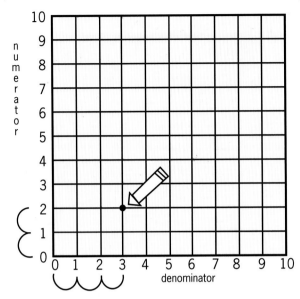

Fractions can be used to find points on a graph. Take the fraction 2/3 for example.

The numerator (2) matches the number along the side of the graph.

The denominator (3) matches the number along the bottom of the graph.

For the fraction 2/3, go up two and over three. It's just that simple.

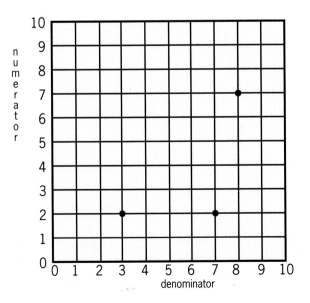

You can use fractions and graph paper to make shapes and pictures.

First, use fractions to find the points on the graph that will make the picture. Make a large dot where each point should be.

What fractions would you use to tell where these points are?

Then connect the points in order to make a picture.

This triangle was made by graphing these fractions and connecting the points in this order:

$\frac{2}{3} \rightarrow \frac{7}{8} \rightarrow \frac{2}{7} \rightarrow \frac{2}{3}$

Use graph paper to draw the following figures. Label your graphs with the numbers 0 through 10 as above. (Note that some of the fractions are proper fractions and some are improper fractions.)

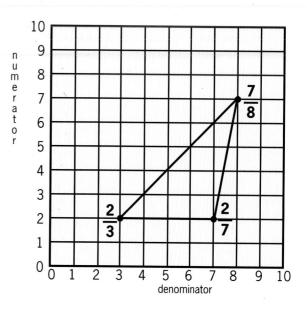

1. $\dfrac{2}{3} \rightarrow \dfrac{2}{6} \rightarrow \dfrac{5}{8} \rightarrow \dfrac{8}{6} \rightarrow \dfrac{8}{3} \rightarrow \dfrac{5}{1} \rightarrow \dfrac{2}{3}$

2. $\dfrac{5}{8} \rightarrow \dfrac{2}{5} \rightarrow \dfrac{4}{5} \rightarrow \dfrac{4}{1} \rightarrow \dfrac{6}{1} \rightarrow \dfrac{6}{5} \rightarrow \dfrac{8}{5} \rightarrow \dfrac{5}{8}$

3. $\dfrac{3}{9} \rightarrow \dfrac{2}{7} \rightarrow \dfrac{2}{6} \rightarrow \dfrac{3}{3} \rightarrow \dfrac{1}{1} \rightarrow \dfrac{3}{2} \rightarrow \dfrac{5}{1} \rightarrow$
$\dfrac{4}{3} \rightarrow \dfrac{5}{6} \rightarrow \dfrac{5}{7} \rightarrow \dfrac{3}{9}$

4. $\dfrac{6}{8} \rightarrow \dfrac{2}{2} \rightarrow \dfrac{8}{4} \rightarrow \dfrac{2}{7} \rightarrow \dfrac{6}{1} \rightarrow \dfrac{6}{8}$

- Now try making a graph picture of your own. Give the fractions to a friend. Have your friend use them to figure out your picture.

Turning Fractions Into Decimals

Any fraction can be turned into a decimal. It's really quite easy. Simply divide the numerator by the denominator. If you use a calculator, it's even easier.

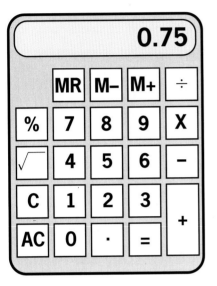

For example, suppose you wanted to change the fraction 3/4 into a decimal. Here's what you would do.

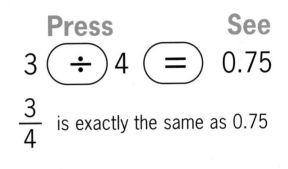

Press   **See**

$3 \div 4 = 0.75$

$\frac{3}{4}$ is exactly the same as 0.75

Why change a fraction into a decimal?

Sometimes it's difficult to tell if one fraction is larger than another. If you change the fractions to decimals, it's easier to compare them.

- Play a little game. Decide which fraction in each pair is larger. Then check by changing each fraction to a decimal. See how many you get right.

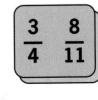

$\frac{4}{7}$ $\frac{2}{3}$ $\frac{5}{8}$ $\frac{7}{12}$ $\frac{3}{4}$ $\frac{8}{11}$ $\frac{9}{16}$ $\frac{3}{5}$

- Turning fractions into decimals can be interesting. See what happens when these ninths fractions are changed into decimals. Look for the pattern. Then finish the sequence without a calculator. When you are finished, use a calculator to check your ideas.

$\dfrac{1}{9}$ = 0.1111111 $\dfrac{5}{9}$ = _____ **?**

$\dfrac{2}{9}$ = 0.2222222 $\dfrac{6}{9}$ = _____ **?**

$\dfrac{3}{9}$ = 0.3333333 $\dfrac{7}{9}$ = _____ **?**

$\dfrac{4}{9}$ = 0.4444444 $\dfrac{8}{9}$ = _____ **?**

- Make a copy of this table of elevenths fractions. Then use a calculator to change each fraction into a decimal. When you are finished look for the pattern. You will be surprised at what you find.

fraction		decimal	fraction		decimal
$\dfrac{1}{11}$	=	0.090909	$\dfrac{6}{11}$	=	_____
$\dfrac{2}{11}$	=	0.181818	$\dfrac{7}{11}$	=	_____
$\dfrac{3}{11}$	=	_____	$\dfrac{8}{11}$	=	_____
$\dfrac{4}{11}$	=	_____	$\dfrac{9}{11}$	=	_____
$\dfrac{5}{11}$	=	_____	$\dfrac{10}{11}$	=	_____

23

Fraction Maze

To get through the maze quickly and easily, first solve the division problems. The answer to each problem tells you which gate to pass through. But you must reduce each answer to its lowest terms. Begin in the center of the maze and come out at the bottom.

A. $\dfrac{1}{2} \div \dfrac{3}{4}$ B. $\dfrac{2}{5} \div \dfrac{1}{3}$ C. $\dfrac{2}{3} \div \dfrac{1}{4}$ D. $\dfrac{1}{4} \div \dfrac{5}{6}$

E. $\dfrac{5}{9} \div \dfrac{5}{8}$ F. $\dfrac{2}{6} \div \dfrac{1}{7}$ G. $\dfrac{2}{6} \div \dfrac{4}{6}$

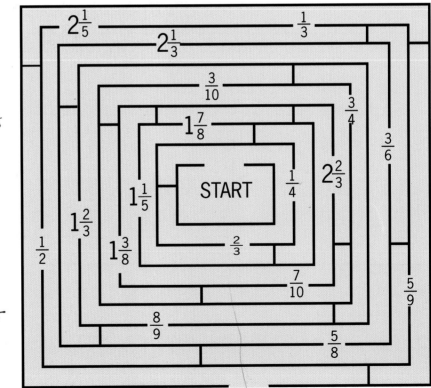

More Fraction Action

See if you can figure out these riddles. You'll need to use a little fraction action to solve them.

The sum of my numerator and denominator is 15.
My denominator is 3 more than my numerator.
What am I?

The fraction 2/3 has an equivalent fraction for which the sum of its numerator and denominator is 25. What's the equivalent fraction?

How many ways can you divide a square into equal halves? Here are three ways.

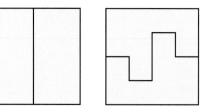 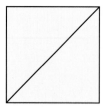

Use some scrap paper or old newspaper to make five squares—about 5 inches on a side. By folding, using a ruler, or by any other means, cut or shade each square into two equal halves. No fair using the examples above.

Folding Fractions

Fold a square piece of paper in half three times, like this:

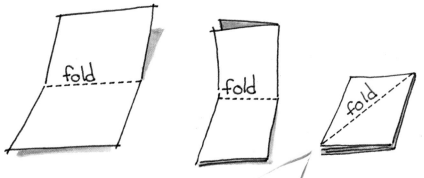

Now unfold the paper an~~~~ it to show how exactly half a squar~~~~ ~~~~ted so that the unpainted half rem~~~~ ~~~~ct square.

How Much?

What part of this large square is s~~~~

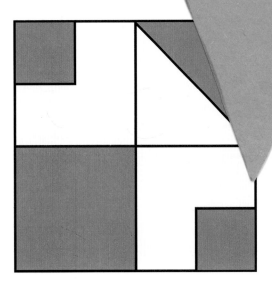

Answers

Pps. 4-5, Alphabet Flags

The L-flag is divided into four equal parts. 2/4 or 1/2 of the flag is black. 2/4 or 1/2 of the flag is yellow.

1/2 of the D-flag is blue. 2/4 or 1/2 of the flag is yellow.

The C-flag is divided into 5 equal parts. 2/5 of the flag is blue, 1/5 of the flag is red, 2/5 of the flag is white.

Pps.6-7, Dividing Shapes

Pps. 8-9, Tangram Puzzle

There are five triangles, one square, and one parallelogram. The seven pieces fit into a square like this.

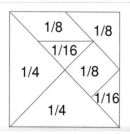

Pps. 10-11, Fraction Card Games

No Answers.

P. 12, Invisible Picture

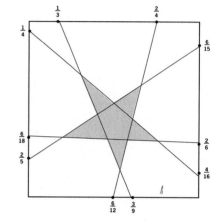

P. 13, Equivalent Fractions Game

No Answers.

P. 14, All Sides Equal

Each side of the triangle has a sum of 1 1/2. Here are three other ways to arrange the fractions so they still add up to 1 1/2.

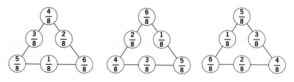

Here are three ways to arrange the numbers 1/3, 2/3, 1, 1 1/3, 1 2/3, and 2 so each side equals 3.

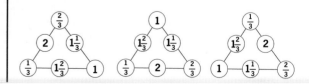

Here's one way to arrange the numbers in the rectangle so the sum of each side equals 3:

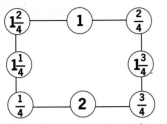

Here's one way to arrange the numbers in the rectangle so the sum of each side equals 3¾:

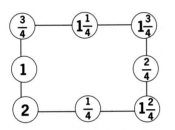

P. 15, Fraction Magic Square

The magic is that the sum of each row, column, and diagonal is 3¾.

1	$2\frac{1}{4}$	$\frac{1}{2}$
$\frac{3}{4}$	$1\frac{1}{4}$	$1\frac{3}{4}$
2	$\frac{1}{4}$	$1\frac{1}{2}$

Pps. 16-17, Fraction Blocks

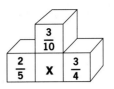

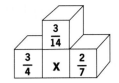

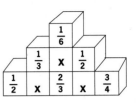

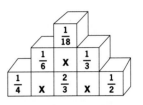

P. 18, Fraction Code

DECODER								
$\frac{1}{4}$	$+$	$\frac{2}{4}$	$=$	$\frac{3}{4}$	$\frac{2}{7}$ $+$ $\frac{3}{7}$ $=$ $\frac{5}{7}$	$\frac{4}{15}$ $+$ $\frac{7}{15}$ $=$ $\frac{11}{15}$
$\frac{1}{3}$	$+$	$\frac{1}{3}$	$=$	$\frac{2}{3}$	$\frac{4}{11}$ $+$ $\frac{5}{11}$ $=$ $\frac{9}{11}$	$\frac{4}{5}$ $-$ $\frac{3}{5}$ $=$ $\frac{1}{5}$
$\frac{7}{8}$	$-$	$\frac{4}{8}$	$=$	$\frac{3}{8}$	$\frac{5}{9}$ $-$ $\frac{3}{9}$ $=$ $\frac{2}{9}$	$\frac{12}{13}$ $-$ $\frac{7}{13}$ $=$ $\frac{5}{13}$
$\frac{15}{20}$	$-$	$\frac{6}{20}$	$=$	$\frac{9}{20}$	$\frac{6}{10}$ $-$ $\frac{3}{10}$ $=$ $\frac{3}{10}$	$\frac{6}{18}$ $+$ $\frac{9}{18}$ $=$ $\frac{15}{18}$
$\frac{5}{12}$	$-$	$\frac{2}{12}$	$=$	$\frac{3}{12}$		$\frac{6}{16}$ $+$ $\frac{3}{16}$ $=$ $\frac{9}{16}$

How long should a cat's legs be?
long enough to touch the ground

What goes up a chimney closed, but can't go down a chimney open?
an umbrella

28

P. 19, Sum and Product Game

sum $= \dfrac{5}{6}$ product $= \dfrac{1}{6}$: $\dfrac{1}{3}$ $\dfrac{1}{2}$

sum $= \dfrac{7}{12}$ product $= \dfrac{1}{12}$: $\dfrac{1}{4}$ $\dfrac{1}{3}$

sum $= 1\dfrac{1}{4}$ product $= \dfrac{3}{8}$: $\dfrac{3}{4}$ $\dfrac{1}{2}$

sum $= 1\dfrac{1}{15}$ product $= \dfrac{4}{15}$: $\dfrac{2}{3}$ $\dfrac{2}{5}$

pps. 20-21, Fraction Graph Pictures

1.)

2.)

3.)

4.)

Pps. 22-23, Turning Fractions Into Decimals

2/3 is larger than 4/7

5/8 is larger than 7/12

3/4 is larger than 8/11

3/5 is larger than 9/16

The decimals for ninths fractions repeat the numerators. The remaining decimals in the sequences are:

5/9 = 0.5555555

6/9 = 0.6666666

7/9 = 0.7777777

8/9 = 0.8888888

This is what your completed elevenths table should look like.

Did you find the patterns?

fraction		decimal	fraction		decimal
$\dfrac{1}{11}$	=	0.090909	$\dfrac{6}{11}$	=	0.545454
$\dfrac{2}{11}$	=	0.181818	$\dfrac{7}{11}$	=	0.636363
$\dfrac{3}{11}$	=	0.272727	$\dfrac{8}{11}$	=	0.727272
$\dfrac{4}{11}$	=	0.363636	$\dfrac{9}{11}$	=	0.818181
$\dfrac{5}{11}$	=	0.454545	$\dfrac{10}{11}$	=	0.909090

The decimals repeat every two digits. The first number increases by one from the smallest fraction to the largest. The second number decreases by one from the smallest to the largest fraction.

29

P. 24, Fraction Maze

A. $^1\!/_2 \div ^3\!/_4 = ^2\!/_3$ B. $^2\!/_5 \div ^1\!/_3 = 1^1\!/_5$

C. $^2\!/_3 \div ^1\!/_4 = 2^2\!/_3$ D. $^1\!/_4 \div ^5\!/_6 = ^3\!/_{10}$

E. $^5\!/_9 \div ^5\!/_8 = ^8\!/_9$ F. $^2\!/_6 \div ^1\!/_7 = 2^1\!/_3$

G. $^2\!/_6 \div ^4\!/_6 = ^1\!/_2$

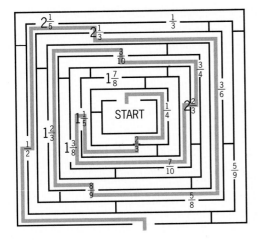

P. 25, More Fraction Action

1. 6/9
2. 10/15

There are an infinite number of ways to divide a square into two equal halves. Here are a few examples:

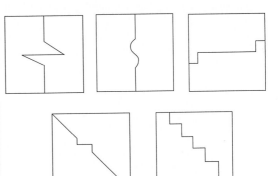

P. 26, Folding Fractions

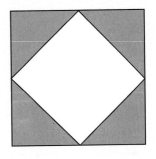

P. 26, How Much?

One half of the large square is shaded.

Glossary

column An up-and-down arrangement of things.

denominator The bottom number in a fraction. In the fraction 3/4, the denominator is 4.

diagonal A line connecting opposite corners of a shape.

divisor A number by which another number is divided.

equivalent fractions Fractions that name the same number or amount.

example: $\dfrac{1}{3}$ $\dfrac{2}{6}$ $\dfrac{3}{9}$

factor Any numbers that, when multiplied together, form a product.

fraction A part of a whole.

hexagon A shape with six sides.

improper fraction A fraction whose numerator is equal to or larger than its denominator.

lowest terms A fraction is in lowest terms if the numerator and denominator have no common factor greater than 1.

numerator The top number in a fraction. In the fraction 3/4, the numerator is 3.

product The answer to a multiplication problem.

$$5 \times 7 = 35$$
product

rectangle A shape with four sides and four right angles.

row A number of objects arranged in a straight line.

square A rectangle with all four sides the same length.

sum The answer to an addition problem.

triangle A shape with three sides.

Index